MW01148323

PREM PRADHAN
APOSTLE TO NEPAL

PREM PRADHAN
APOSTLE TO NEPAL

A MAN AS GREAT AS THE HIMALAYANS

SeedSowers Publishing
Jacksonville, Florida

Prem Pradhan:
Apostle to Nepal
Copyright © 2008
Seedsowers

Published by SeedSowers
Christian Books Publishing House
4003 N Liberty Street
Jacksonville, FL 32206
www.seedsowers.com
800-228-2665

Printed in the United States of America

ISBN 13: 978-0-9797515-4-7
       10:    -0-9797515-4-3

Table of Contents

Chronology of Prem's Life

1924   Birth

1954–1960   Prem Began His Ministry

1960–1965   First Imprisonment (6 years)

1965–1971   Planting Churches in Nepal

1971–1974   Second Imprisonment (3 years)

1974–1977   Growth of Work in Nepal

1977–1979   Third Imprisonment
               (Served 13 Months of 60-year Sentence)

1979–1998   Prem's Planting of Churches Starts Over
               after British and American Missionaries
               Steal His Churches

1998   Death

The God who made the Himalayan Mountains
matched that feat when He made Prem Pradhan.

If you have the faith of a mustard seed,
you can say to that mountain, "Move!"
and that mountain will move.
For forty years, Prem Pradhan
moved the Himalayans.

xiii

If you preach a faith other than the one into which you were born, you will be imprisoned for three years.

If you baptize anyone, you will be sentenced to six years in prison.

Anyone who is baptized will be imprisoned for one year for being baptized.

This is what Prem Pradhan faced. In forty years' time, he was imprisoned for eleven years; and 20,000 Christians went to prison for a year for being baptized!

Before he died, there had been over 500 churches in Nepal from his ministry.

Here is the story of the man who moved the Himalayans.

Prem Pradhan's Testimony
Fort Erie, Ontario

Other than this testimony, there is no written autobiography of Prem Pradhan. Perhaps the longest and most detailed testimony was this one, given by him in Fort Erie, Ontario, Canada in 1989. The testimony given at that time was thorough, but the reader will keep in mind that this autobiography is limited in the information about the remaining nine years of Pradhan's life after this testimony was given.

1

Prem Pradhan's Testimony

Conversion Experience

I come from the little country of Nepal and was born in a Hindu family. In my time, schools did not exist in my country. There was only one high school in Nepal. There were no roads. My parents sent me to a Hindu mission school in Calcutta where I was educated. While I was there, the Second World War started, and most of our people in Nepal were recruited in the British army. We were the most famous soldiers, the world-renown "Gurkhas." I, too, was recruited in the Royal Air Force.

Throughout the time of the war, I served in the Air Force. When World War II ended, I went home and was a standby for the Air Force as required. At that time, I did not know Jesus. India received her independence and I was called back to India to work in the tank regiment. A new tank regiment was started with the mountain people and I joined them. And still I did not know Jesus.

In 1951, while I was on leave, I first heard about Jesus in a street meeting in Darjeeling, India. Darjeeling borders the eastern part of Nepal along the same mountain range. There were Christians in Darjeeling who were Nepalese, but they held Indian citizenship, so they had the freedom to have churches. My family at that time, which consisted of my grandfather, lived in the eastern part of Nepal. The shortest route I could take to go from Darjeeling, India to my home in eastern Nepal required a three-day walk. My uncle lived in Darjeeling and had a business there, so I went there and stayed with him.

One Saturday I went to the market and found a group of people singing songs. I stood and listened. After that, someone started to preach the gospel. This small group that preached the gospel was established by Bakht Singh. The group was made up of a few Christians from four or five families. All the members of the family went out to preach the gospel. They preached that it is appointed for a man to die once and after that comes judgment. Also, for those whose name is not found in the book of life, they will be cast into the lake of fire where they are tormented forever and ever without escape.

I was born a Hindu and was educated in the Ram Krishna Mission School (which was a Hindu mission school) in Calcutta. All the teachers were Sadhus and Gurus. They taught us all the good things about the religion and told us not to do evil. They warned us that if any man did evil, he could be reincarnated as an animal or insect in his next 54,000 cycles of life; so one must do good. But sometimes I did wrong as a student and felt remorseful. I went to my teachers and asked them if a man did wrong and was reincarnated as an animal or insect, what could an animal or insect do in order to become a man again? However, my teachers always told me to sit down, and so I got no answer. I did learn one thing from them, and that is, the soul will not die. It will go to the place of punishment or return to where it came from. So, when I heard the Christians preaching on the street that day, teaching the same thing but in a different way, it was in my heart to ask them if they knew the answer for man to escape eternal punishment.

These Christians invited me to visit them the next day. It was a Sunday and they worshiped in a home. They gave me the address and I went. I sat for two to three hours while they sang and had their meeting. After that, one of them asked me what I wanted to know. I asked them to explain to me how man can escape the eternal punishment which they were preaching about. I was taken to another room with three brothers. They sat down and prayed. Then, opening their Bibles, they showed me the

4

verses which told of God's plan for salvation. These brothers showed me from the Bible that when we ask God for forgiveness, he will forgive us and will remember our sins no more. I learned that God forgave me of all my sins, so I was happy.

These Christians also sold me a Bible and showed me how to read it. I was told to read the Gospel of John seven times and then the New Testament seven times before going on to the Old Testament. Having nothing to do, since I was on leave, I read the Gospel of John and finished it seven times before going on to the New Testament. That is how I started to read the Bible.

Every evening the Christians had meetings and prayer meetings in someone's home. I would go and have fellowship with them. That helped me to grow as a Christian. When the time came, I told these Christians that I needed to return to my work. They encouraged me to be baptized. Having explained to me what baptism was, they took me to the river in the valley close to the town of Darjeeling and baptized me. I returned home and went back to work in the army the next day.

While I was with the Christians in Darjeeling, I learned from them by joining them every Saturday to preach the gospel and give out tracts to people. When I returned to the army, I started to share with people that I was a Christian. They asked me many questions which I found difficult to answer. For example, they asked me if I was a Catholic. I answered that I did not know. Some asked me if I was a Protestant. I answered that I did not know. Others in my unit asked me if I was a Baptist. I told them, "I read about John the Baptist, but I do not know what I am. I just finished the New Testament seven times and I must start with the Old Testament. It is so big I have not finished it yet."

I wrote a letter to the brother who baptized me and who was working as postmaster in the Darjeeling Post Office. I told him of my experience in the army and the questions people were asking me. He wrote back and quoted a verse in Acts 11:26 which said that the disciples were called "Christians" for the first time in Antioch. "So, brother, you are not a Catholic nor a Protestant, but just a simple Christian."

Thank God that today I am still a simple Christian and I do not know any other thing.

Prem's Call to the Ministry

I continued my time in the army, and every year during my two months leave, I went back to this small group of Christians. They were increasing in number each year. I fellowshipped with them and helped in some gospel work, up to the border of Nepal. When the leave was over, I was back again in the army.

One night God spoke to me: "Prem, go back to your own people and preach the gospel to them." I found it hard to accept that because I was a major in the army and was a young man. I saw that the small group of Christians who were preaching the gospel had no job, no money, and not much clothes. They were poor. I was a major in the army, earning good money, and I did not want to give it up.

Every month I sent my tithes to the church in Darjeeling. That month I sent half of my salary. With the gift, I wrote to the brothers who baptized me and told them to send someone to Nepal to preach the gospel. This brother understood that something must have happened to me. He wrote back thanking me for the gift, but told me that if God had called me to Nepal, they could not send someone else.

Once again I struggled with it, because I loved being in the army and did not want to give up my job. When I read the Bible, God spoke to me through His Word. When I prayed, God spoke in my heart to go back to my own people. I found that very hard, so I stopped reading the Bible and praying altogether. For fifteen days I struggled, and at night I could not sleep. At last I decided to go. I wrote a resignation letter, fell on my bed, and told the Lord that I would go. I did it so that I might be able to get some sleep, for I had not slept for fifteen days. That night I slept well.

In the morning I went to my colonel and handed in my resignation. The colonel said to me, "Prem, you are young, only 27 years old. You are a major and have good chances of promotion. Why are you doing this? Take your resignation letter back." I replied that I could not do that. I told him the truth about God's calling me to return to Nepal and how for fifteen days I struggled and could not sleep. The colonel accepted my resignation letter and it took another three months before I was released from the army.

When I left the army, I went back to the small group of Christians in Darjeeling. One of the brothers prayed for me and said, "Brother Prem, we are happy that you are back, but if you return to Nepal you will be imprisoned. It is better that you work among the Nepalese here. All the churches here are Nepalese."

I told them, "God called me to preach the gospel in Nepal. I know the law says that if anyone is a Christian he faces a one-year imprisonment, and if anyone preaches the gospel it is a three-year imprisonment, and if anyone baptizes somebody it is a six-year imprisonment. I know that. But Jesus spoke to my heart to go back to my own people."

I worked for awhile in Darjeeling and the surrounding areas, where the Lord helped me to establish three churches in three months. The brothers were very happy that these new churches were established on the Nepal-Darjeeling border, but God kept speaking to me to go back to my own people, and I decided to return.

2

Preaching the Gospel in Nepal

Upon my return to Nepal, I started to tell people about Jesus. It was very different preaching the gospel in Nepal compared to Darjeeling. The people of Darjeeling have been under the rule of the British, so they were exposed to many things. But not so in Nepal, for the country had never been occupied by people from another nation. I talked to the people about a man who died and was raised again three days later. I spoke of how He did many good works, healing the sick, preaching the kingdom of God, and of how man can escape eternal punishment. He was the only man who died and was raised from the dead, unlike our gods who died and none was raised from the dead. Even Buddha, who was born in Nepal in 500 B.C., died.

Most of the Nepalese people are Buddhists, and the king is a Hindu. The state religion is Hinduism. I told the people that the Buddhist temple was dead. Buddha died and those who are dead cannot answer the living. Jesus was the only one who died and was raised from the dead; and when I talked to Him, He answered me. I also told them how Jesus sent me to tell them the message of salvation, and how they could escape eternal punishment. All the people in my country knew that if they did evil, they would be punished from one life to another by being reincarnated as an animal or insect for 54,000 cycles of life.

I shared with the people how they could escape this eternal punishment by accepting Jesus as their personal Savior and confessing their sins. Then they would know the forgiveness of their sins and be changed into a new man.

Jesus said, "Go, preach the gospel, heal the sick. Freely you have received, freely give." I told the people that if anyone was sick, I would pray for them and that Jesus would heal them, because He promised to do that. Sometimes when the people asked me to pray for the sick, I prayed and God healed them. In my country, the sick would go to the witch doctors, the priests and the Llamas. These men sacrificed animals and charged the people money. They prayed for the sick and some got healed sometimes. But I did not charge the people anything, nor was it necessary to have people pay for sacrifices. When the people saw that Jesus healed, they believed.

Those that believed, I taught them more and prepared them that they might be willing to suffer. The reason the people became Christians and were willing to suffer was because they knew they could escape eternal punishment and be in heaven after their death. This was something that was very real to them because of their old beliefs. Also, they learned that they could have fellowship with God in this life and that He could keep them from evil.

When the people saw the miracles of healing, they accepted Jesus and were changed by Him. Then they began to encounter suffering, first from their own family. I taught them what Jesus taught in the Bible: that believers would suffer from their own family and that their own relatives would be against them. Sometimes when people became Christians they were not allowed to draw water from the spring that others used. So, Christians faced suffering right from the beginning.

When the Christians grew a little stronger in spirit (through suffering persecution from families and relatives) and they were able to resist and be strong in their faith, I taught them about baptism. I made known to them the penalty of the law in Nepal, whereby they could face imprisonment for a year.

When believers were ready to face imprisonment and suffer, I took them down to the river. Getting into the waters first, I would challenge them, "You must think again. If today you were asked to be in prison, not because of any wrong you have done, would you go willingly and cheerfully?" When they said they were ready for that, then they would come one by one into the waters and I would baptize them in the river.

After baptism, we broke bread together, and I would go to another place. I left these believers with the Gospel of John, in the hands of a brother who could read a little. It usually takes about two to three weeks to preach the gospel, and when some people were converted, I stayed with them all the time. Knowing that I had to leave for another place, I tried from the very beginning to find a man who could read. Then I could entrust the group to him. So if he was a farmer, I went to his farm. If he tended the cows in the forest, I remained with him to teach him.

In these villages where I worked, I stayed in a brother's home. In Nepal people were very open and hospitable. If I came into a village, someone would surely open their home and I would stay with them. If there were no Christians, I would stay with anyone who would receive me into their home. However, it was difficult to stay in the home of someone who was not a Christian because every home had a family god. Although the people gave me food, they found it hard to keep me in their homes because I was a Christian. Their family gods might be offended. So, they would give me a place where they kept the cattle, and I slept on the straw. Sometimes when I was not able to reach a village, then I climbed up a tree and spent the night there because of the tigers and leopards.

I prayed very much on these trips and carried as little as possible with me on my travels: perhaps just a change of clothes. Because of the journey through the mountains, little things became heavier and heavier as you climbed up, and it was tiring. Even the Bibles became heavy. When people became Christians, I left the Gospel of John with them so they could read and grow spiritually. I traveled everywhere on foot and always alone.

Because I needed to draw my pension from the army, which was in the Darjeeling area, I went back and fellow-shipped in the churches there. I told them of the things that were going on in Nepal. They prayed much for me and were happy to learn that there were people in Nepal who became Christians, who were baptized and broke bread together. They rejoiced because they had prayed much for me.

It usually took about three months before I was able to return to the churches that were started. Sometimes it might take six months to a year. When I got back there, I found that not only was the church still there, but they had increased everywhere. It was a beautiful thing. The people who had believed told others that Jesus was alive.

Believers learned from the beginning that Jesus told us to pray for the sick. I told them that it was not just a man like me who could pray and see God heal. I had taught believers that they were members of Christ's body and He is the head. Just as they had seen me pray and Jesus healed, now that they are members of His body they, too, could pray and ask God to heal if any sick were brought to them. They could gather together and pray and Jesus would heal. So they practiced it. When others saw the healing that took place, they too believed and were added to the small group of believers. It might begin with just four or five. Next time around they might have increased to eight or ten. And so believers increased in that way.

The Buddhists and the Hindus, who charged much money from the poor for their prayers and sacrifices, also witnessed that the sick recovered from the prayers of Christians. Not only did the Christians charge nothing from those who brought their sick, but they even tried to feed the sick person and those who brought him, though they themselves were poor. There might be just four or five Christians, but still they shared their food with them. They showed practical love to them. When the sick who were healed regained their strength, then they returned to their homes which might be in another village. So a church would be started in another village, and when I came back, I would go to visit the new converts.

We must not only talk about the gospel, but we must live it.

We have two hundred different tribes and twelve different languages. The customs and cultures are different from one another. We must work in the way that is suitable to my country. Then only can churches be established. I do not speak the twelve different languages. I speak the common language of Nepal and my own tribal language (the Niwar tribe). There are eleven other tribal languages, but the Niwar people live all over the country because they are business people, and they have businesses everywhere.

I went first to the Niwar people and God helped me. I told them the story of how I heard of a man that died and was raised again. When the people heard this, many wanted to know where this man was and where it happened, and so on. In this way I created curiosity in the hearts of the people. When they asked me questions, other people also heard the answers, and some became Christians. These who believed were from other tribes, but they heard the message in the common language. Although they did not know my tribal language and I did not know theirs, we all spoke the common language. So it was in this way that God helped me.

In 1954, I started preaching in Nepal, and I was put in prison in 1960. During those six years, there were fifty-four Christians with eight churches established in different places. However, due to my disobedience to God in those first three months when He first called me, I did not see any souls saved during the first three years. All those years I traveled and wept and prayed, but I was not able to win one soul because I had disobeyed God for three months. God broke me. He taught me that I could not do anything. So when I learned helplessness in myself, and that Jesus alone could work through me, then God began to work.

I spent all those three years alone with much hardship because I had not given myself up in the beginning. It was the hardest time. At times I crossed the same river a hundred times a day in order to follow it to reach another village. I would be soaking wet. Still the Lord would help me, protecting me from the wild tigers when I came across them face-to-face. I shared the gospel everywhere, but no one asked me to pray. Only after three years did one man ask me to pray for his mother who was paralyzed for six years.

I prayed. She was healed, and that was the beginning of the church.

So I say surely that when God tells us to do something, it is very hard to disobey. If we do, we may be punished like I was. After I had preached the gospel in one place, I went to another. (No addresses were kept as is done in the West, because people did not have addresses.)

In 1960, I was in a place far from anywhere that had any Christians. The nearest church was about a three-day walk away. God spoke to me, "Prem go back." He gave me the name of the place. (This is where the first group of Christians was later imprisoned.) He told me to go back to these people because there was going to be a severe persecution in the church. He told me that I would be imprisoned for six years.

It was a very hard thing to learn that I would be in prison for six years and that Christians would also be imprisoned. My mind was heavy with the thought: if I went back, I would be imprisoned for six years. What God had spoken to me He would fulfill. I could have left the country, because I was in a place that was close to the border. The devil tempted me with many things in my heart. But the first three years, when I struggled with the work because of my disobedience, had taught me many things. It was a good lesson. So I refused everything that the devil tempted me with. I did not run away. I read the Word of God and found out that only the hirelings would run away when the sheep were attacked by wild animals, because they were not their own sheep. But these people were my own sheep. I could not run away.

3

Prem's First Imprisonment and Ministry in Prison

I went back to the place where the persecution started and to the people who were in police custody. I went to the police station and was told by the police officers that if I confessed that there were no Christians, I could leave and the people would be released, and we could continue to worship in the home. I would have to give them a written statement saying there were no Christians. I could not do that because it would rock the church and tear up all the nine Christians (four women and five men). One by one, the police officers tried their best to get the nine to say that they were not Christians, hoping one might give in. They did many things to tempt them to deny the faith, but no one denied Jesus.

At last the police officer called me and said, "We have tried, but no one is willing to deny Jesus. How do you teach them, since they are not educated and only one of them can read?" I replied that what the people heard from me, they believed and practiced. When they did this, they came to know God personally themselves. They could not deny what they knew, so that is why they could not deny Jesus.

All of us Christians were sent to court. The court decided that the nine would get a year's imprisonment and I would get a six-year imprisonment.

All the nine Christians were sent to prison. One of the women was pregnant at that time, and her child was born in prison after a month. Another had a twenty-one-day-old daughter with her. Still another woman had two sons.

Conditions in Prison

There was not much room in the prison. The cell was about fifteen feet by twelve feet, and there were fifteen people in that cell. It had one door and no windows. It had a tin roof and dirt floor. The government does not provide any cooked food. Everyone received a half pound of rice and each had to cook their own. All cooking utensils and blankets had to be taken from home into the prison. Should anyone become sick, no medication was provided. There were no rest rooms in the cell. Every night when the door was closed, the people who were locked up for twelve to fourteen hours in one room had to arrange their own means. People became ill in the prison. Some contracted tuberculosis and diarrhea and it was a little difficult! Due to over crowdedness in one room, many people died in prison because of tuberculosis infections. We had to cook our food in the cell and sleep there as well. On one side of the cell we made a hole in the ground where people could stand in line to cook their own meals. This meant that there was smoke in the cell all the time.

That is the way we lived in the prison.

Every day we were told that if we denied Jesus we could return home, but no one denied Him. Every one of the Christians served a full year in the prison. After that they were released. God protected the mother and the child that was born in prison. The boy, who was named Isheri, "begot from God," has now finished high school and completed Bible school.

I sent Isheri to India. He established a church there and worked with the elders. Then he returned to college to finish his Bachelor of Education, because he wanted to be a teacher. I sent him to college so that he could help in my school. The little girl who was twenty-one days old when her mother was sent to prison has now finished high school, three years of Bible school, and is now working in a government hospital. She is a very good nurse and is bringing many who work with her to Christ.

Jail-Break

After all the nine Christian brothers and sisters were released, I alone was left in prison. Nepal at that time had an uprising. It was around the end of 1961 and the beginning of 1962. Many communist and other political parties were banned, and many people were put in prison. Those who were in charge of the prison rooms (prison trustees) met together. They were to report to the government if anything happened.

One day some guns were smuggled into the prison. A man who was a communist and a political prisoner came to my room with a rifle. He asked me to join his group in an escape. I was tempted by the thought: Here is the opportunity for you to go free; if you go now, you will skip another five years that is left of your imprisonment. It was very difficult for me to decide. However, in my spirit I reasoned with myself: If you go, you will never be able to come back to Nepal; you will lose everything and the sheep will be scattered. I finally told the men that I could not go with them. The man who had the rifle said that he would kill me. He loaded his rifle, pointed it at me and counted to three to fire. I closed my eyes and prayed,

"Lord, if it is Thy will, take me home, but if not, protect me." Then a verse came to my mind from Psalms 34:7, "The angel of the Lord encampeth round about them that fear Him and delivers them." After that, I felt strongly that God was going to protect me. At the count of three, the man with the rifle pressed the trigger. The first bullet did not leave the barrel of the rifle, so the man loaded the rifle again. This time the bullet fell out. He loaded it once more and said, "The first bullet might miss you, but not the second. You have a chance to change your mind and join us."

All this happened very quickly.

I was strengthened in my heart because of God's Word and felt sure that He was going to protect me. The man fired the second round, but it did not touch me. I could feel the hot air as it shot past my right ear, hit the wall and bounced back. It hit the leg of the man with the rifle. It broke his leg and he fell, wounded.

I told them that it would be very difficult for them to escape. They had a long way to go, crossing mountains and valleys to get into India. If the army captured them, they would lose their lives. It would be better for them to leave me and go. Another man took the rifle from the man who was wounded, left him lying there, and left the prison.

Many other prisoners saw the jailbreak but did not know what was happening. They saw people leaving and so they also tried to join them, taking their own things with them. I felt very burdened in my heart, as I thought of the many prisoners who had been in prison for many years. They were weak and some were sick and could not run. If the police and the army came, they would surely be killed.

I went to my room, took a small lock from a box that I had and locked the door from the inside. I told the prisoners not to go because the government was not freeing them; it was a jailbreak. The police would soon come, and all would be shot and killed if they were caught leaving. So the prisoners stayed.

The prison where we were was situated halfway down the slope of a mountain. Higher up on the slope were the army and police barracks and the district headquarters for the government office. The prison was about a mile-and-a half down from them, so when the police and the army came, we could see from the prison that they were coming. They chased the prisoners who escaped, and many who could not walk were killed or injured. The rest were brought back to the prison again. I told all the prisoners that remained in the prison to get back into their rooms so that they might avoid being shot by the police and the army. I locked the door and stood outside at the gate. A police officer and an army officer, together with the district magistrate, came to the gate of the prison and asked me how the jail was broken because the door was locked.

I told them that the gate was broken into and some were gone. They asked me why I did not go with the others. I told them that I was a Christian and that I would not break the law, nor had I any intention to cause any harm: so why should I join them? The police officer knew that I was once an army man, and that I could have escaped with them. I told him that I did not want to escape because I did not want to break the law. I was in prison for breaking the law because I obeyed the law of God, which was a different matter. In obeying the law of God which told me to tell people about Christ, I broke the government's law. But I told them I did not want to break the law of the country. Then the officers asked me if there were any men left inside the prison. I told them that there were many inside and that I had locked them in a room with my own lock to save their lives. I explained how I told the prisoners that if they left, they would surely die, since the police did not know who were the communists and who were not.

At that time many who were shot and injured were brought outside the prison and were beaten. I asked the authorities not to beat them, because the prisoners were innocent: they only left because the gate was open. What was to be gained in being so harsh and so cruel to them. The authorities asked me to help them to count the rest of the people that were left in prison, and I told them that they must not beat them because they were innocent. I counted them and there were more than two hundred people who were gone from the prison.

Of those who were brought back, many died and the rest were kept in prison. This incident helped me to convert many people.

Beginning of Prem's Ministry While in Prison

During our first year in prison, we did not try to convert anyone. Some of the other prisoners learned that we were Christians from hearing us sing songs. The five brothers who had been arrested with me were interested in studying the New Testament. During that one year, we studied through the New Testament three times. It was beautiful. I learned much more studying the Bible in prison, because everything Jesus said (that we have to suffer from family and the world) had all come true. What Paul wrote to Christians about suffering became real for us. The Bible became alive because we were suffering the same things that were written. We had great joy in learning.

Many sang songs, "Rejoice in the Lord always, and again I say rejoice," quoting what Paul wrote, without understanding that when Paul wrote these verses he was in prison. He wrote Philippians while he was in chains, and in that situation he told others to rejoice. He had a reason for that. It is really true that physical torture is painful. No physical torture is good. But we learned, as Christians in prison, that torture can only hurt the physical body; the soul and spirit are free. Also, we read again and again in God's Word that we have our reward in heaven. Actually, I feel we also have it on earth. When by my suffering someone was brought to the Lord and I was able to win souls, it gave me the greatest joy in my heart. When I saw the condition of man, then I also saw why all suffering helped to win people to the Lord. When one soul was won to the Lord, it was a great joy to see how he changed.

This is the greatest joy any man can have. In spite of physical torture, suffering helped me.

Prison conditions were very difficult, with poor food, bed bugs, lice and mice, mosquitoes at night and over crowdedness. The Christians suffered much. Despite that, they endured, and they were released after a year. I remained in prison because I had a six-year sentence. I told the Lord that I was a little lonely because I had never cooked before. When the brothers were with me in prison, we cooked and ate together. When I was a little boy, I had stayed in a boarding school in Calcutta and I ate my meals in the school. In the army, I never cooked. Even when I traveled to preach the gospel, I never cooked because I carried nothing with me. People would give me food or I purchased it. But now the brothers had left the prison and I had to cook my own food. It was a difficult thing to build a fire with two small pieces of wood. The smoke would fill the room. So I prayed, "Lord, help me. How can I spend another five years in this way?" The Lord spoke to me saying, "There are many people with you. Why not have a church here?"

So, I started to share the gospel (which I had not done during the first year) to win men to Christ. Slowly I began to talk to the prisoners, and I also helped them in practical ways. I took care of those that were sick, and in that way I won souls to Christ in the prison. When people became Christian, it encouraged me and we helped each other. The new Christians began to help other prisoners, caring for the sick, donating blood, cooking food for them, and so on.

Many people died in prison because when they were sick they could not cook their own food, and they had no medicine. The Christians helped the sick and encouraged them and prayed for them, and more prisoners became Christian. Someone reported this fact to the prison authorities. The authorities came and tried to identify those prisoners who had become Christians by asking them to raise their hands. When the jailer found out that many of the prisoners had become Christians, he became angry at me.

"You make people Christians outside the prison, so we put you in prison. Now you convert them inside the prison. We will deal with you after we have taken care of these Christians first."

The prison authorities took all the Christians outside and they were beaten severely. They were bleeding, and some who were unconscious were dragged back into the prison again. Not all the Christians in prison raised their hands to identify themselves. Some, being young in the faith, feared punishment. So these who remained unidentified helped me to take the wounded back to their rooms. We cleaned them with water and anything else that we could use. And we prayed for them. In that way, we tried to revive them back to their senses. When they regained consciousness, we all gathered together in one place to pray. We asked the Lord to help those who had been badly beaten and wounded, and to heal them and give them strength.

After prayer, I told the Christians that I was really sorry that they were so severely beaten and wounded. They said, "Brother Prem, you taught us that we have to suffer, and we thank God that he has counted us worthy to suffer." How this encouraged my heart! What I had taught now came into their lives. They had not rejected it nor denied it. Rather, they suffered and rejoiced. It strengthened me to see that what I taught was received by these prisoners who had become Christians. Even when they suffered for Christ, they still followed Him.

The next day the jailers called for me. Before I left, I told the Christian brothers, "I am leaving now, and I do not know what they are going to do to me. Please pray for me, all of you."

They prayed for me and I left with the jailer. He looked at me angrily. He told me, "We have decided not to keep you in prison with all the other prisoners. We will keep you outside."

The jailer ordered a man to put me in chains, both my hands and my feet, the right hand to the right foot and the left hand to the left foot.

Persecution in Prison

Many people died in prison, and the bodies were kept in a small room outside the wall. The families of the dead were then notified. The news would take about four to five days to reach them and another four or five days for the families to come and claim the dead. Meanwhile, the dead bodies were kept in a little room, usually from seven to ten days. Sometimes no one came to claim the dead bodies. Eventually they were thrown to the dogs and the vultures.

I was taken to that room. I only had my blankets. In that room with the dead bodies in it, I was to continue my

imprisonment. There was a horrible odor. Bones were
everywhere. I cleaned up one corner a little and placed my
blanket down. I sat there and prayed in my heart. Then a
passage of Scripture came to me about the persecution of
Stephen (Acts 7). When Stephen was giving his testimony,
he suddenly saw the heavens opened and Jesus standing at
the right hand of the Father. As he recounted what he saw,
all the Jews and the council condemned him to death, and
he was stoned. About the time of his death, the persecution
of the church began, and the Christians left Jerusalem.
Wherever they went they established churches. Only the
apostles remained in Jerusalem. Saul went into homes
seeking out men and women to put into prison. Later, Saul
acquired a letter from the high priest and went to Damascus
to seek out Christians, in order to bring them back to prison
in Jerusalem. The story went on to recount how Saul, when
nearing Damascus, saw a great light and fell to the ground.
He heard a voice saying, "Saul, Saul, why are you persecuting Me?" Baffled, Saul asked, "Who are you Lord?"
The voice said, "I am Jesus whom you are persecuting."

I stopped at that point and started thinking. Saul was
not persecuting Jesus, Saul was persecuting Christians.
That was about fourteen years, I think, after Jesus' resurrection. Jesus came to meet Saul on the road to Damascus
asking, "Saul, Saul why are you persecuting Me?" He did
not say, "Saul, Saul why are you persecuting Christians?"

That helped me to realize that Jesus not only saved my soul and one day I will be in heaven, but He loved me so much that even when I was in this place (this small room where the dead bodies are kept, with all the bad odor and me in chains), He was willing to be with me and to suffer my pain in His own body. I just rejoiced over that!

How great is our God, the creator of the heavens and the earth, and yet He is happy to be with me in my body, taking my pain in His body. Realizing that, I rejoiced and cried out all the louder, giving thanks to God. The guard, upon hearing me, asked whom I was talking to. I told him I was talking to Jesus. He asked, "How did Jesus get in? I am on duty here." He did not believe me and opened the door, searching for this Jesus with his flashlight. Not finding anyone in the room he said, "Jesus is not here." I told him how Jesus was with me and how I first found Him when I was a sinner and He forgave my sins. He took all my old nature in His body to the Cross, and now He was living in me. I told the guard that he could find Jesus too. He asked me more questions, and I told him how he could find Jesus and have peace in his own heart. The man laid down his rifle, opened the door and knelt down and prayed, asking God to forgive him of his sins. So he became a Christian.

What a joy for me to know that even in chains in this place of decaying bodies, no one could stop God from working. But we have to suffer, we have to pay the price. God cannot work without man. That is why He needs men who are willing to suffer. He uses them. Yes, we suffer, but God knows each one of us. And according to how much suffering we can endure, He will give that much. He will not give us suffering beyond our capacity. That is how God gives grace along with the suffering: He gives us the grace to suffer. That is what I have learned from my own experience and the experiences of other believers.

During the time that I was placed in the room with the dead for six months, I was in chains. I had no change of clothes because it was all tattered and gone. I did not shave and had no baths, so lice were born on my body, making many wounds everywhere. The guards who became Christians brought water and cleaned me. They gave me clothes, but I was unable to wear them because of the chains on my hands and feet. The chains were never taken off during the entire six months that I was kept in that room. The brothers who became Christians in prison cooked my rice and sent it to me once a day. Physically, I had some problems because of my leg. It swelled up because of the wounds.

All the four guards who watched me became Christians. When the jailer discovered that, he wrote a letter to the capital city, asking the government what they should do with me. They were told to send me to the maximum security prison in the northern part of Nepal.

In that place prisoners served lifetime imprisonment or were executed. The jailer said to me, "You make people Christians outside, so we put you inside the prison. You make people Christians inside the prison, so we put you in that little room outside the prison. Even there, you made the guards become Christians. We thought you would die in four or five days in this room with the dead. We gave you a maximum of fifteen days to live, but after six months you are still alive. We do not want you anymore, so we will send you to another prison."

So they removed the chains to send me to the next prison. I thanked the jailer before leaving.

Transfer from Prison to Prison

I was transferred from the first prison, and my foot and leg were badly injured because of the chains. It took me seven days to walk to the next prison. It was called Sanga. There were about two hundred prisoners there. I was classified as a dangerous prisoner because I won prisoners and guards to Christ. They kept me in stocks in the open field outside the prison, close to the guard's room. They did this sometimes, to try to find out about dangerous prisoners before letting them in. If they died while being exposed outside, they just got rid of the prisoner's body.

When they kept me outside, it was winter time and that actually helped me because of the snow. All my wounds were washed clean by the snow. Being exposed to the sun's light, the wounds healed quickly. I stayed in the snow for fifteen days outside the prison building.

One day the chief guard came and asked me, "What is your crime?" I told him that I was a Christian. Then he asked me what a Christian was. I told him that if I were to die, then I would be in heaven. He replied, "That is not a crime; I thought you had killed many people." I told him, "Oh, no, Sir, I did not kill anyone; I saved many." So the chief guard told me that he would talk to the jailer and have me put back inside the prison along with other prisoners. (He preferred to put me inside, because while keeping me on the outside, the guards were given extra duty, since in the night someone was always assigned to guard me.)

So I was put back inside the prison once again. All the other prisoners started asking me how I survived, because those that were kept outside were mostly hanged. Since I was back in prison, they wanted to know what my crime was. I told them that I was a Christian. When they asked me what a Christian was, I shared with them and showed them how they could be Christians too. That was how other prisoners learned of the gospel. When I prayed for them, they were healed and they became Christians.

Once again, in that prison, those new believers learned to sing songs and rejoice. When I got a group of Christians, we would have Bible studies together. Others joined in. We had a good time. But when the jailer learned once again that other prisoners became Christian, they moved me to yet another prison. I stayed in the second prison for only four months.

The third prison to which I was sent was called Chuncha. It was a small prison of only about fifty people. I did not stay there long either, because the same thing happened. People became Christians the same way when I talked to them, and so I was moved again to another prison. It was called Pocra and had about three to four hundred people. The prison authorities decided that I should not be kept with the male prisoners, so they put me with the women prisoners.

In Nepal, the men go into the army for two to three years, including married men. Sometimes, during a festival where all the villagers gathered together for bartering and celebration, the women whose husbands had left them to go into the army stayed together with other men. Some of these women had children outside of their legal marriage. In Nepal, women could be punished by law for immorality. Women who do not keep faith with their husbands can be imprisoned. Also at that time in Nepal, there was a caste system. Someone from a higher caste could marry a person from the lower caste, but a woman could be imprisoned for marrying outside her caste. Today the caste system has been abolished. These are some of the reasons why there were women in prisons.

It was very difficult for me to remain with the women prisoners as the only man. I was criticized for everything I did. I kept quiet and prayed in my heart, "Lord, help me to win some souls." As I stayed there, slowly the Lord helped me, and some were won to Christ.

When these women became Christians, they were truly and completely changed. They learned Christian songs. Gradually the group grew to a good number of people.

The Nepalese love to sing. They make up songs and sing them to each other, and by songs they communicate to one another. They are very musically inclined. When the girls go to cut grass in the forest, one group on one side of the mountain will sing to another group working on another side of the mountain. The latter then sings back to the first group in reply. They make up these songs easily, and through songs they speak to one another. Our people love songs, and even the young boys and girls talk to one another from one mountain to another by singing. For instance, a man sings and asks me something, and I answer back in a song. People love to sing, and every tribe in every area have their specific kind of songs; so the songs differ in each region.

In a church meeting, someone may begin with a song and the rest will join in. That is the way we worship.

When the jailer learned that the new converts had left their old songs and started singing Christian songs, he realized that even the women had become Christians.

It was no use keeping me in that prison either, so they moved me to yet another prison. In every prison the same thing occurred. In this way the Lord help me to win many.

At different times I was sent to different areas to continue my imprisonment. In the summertime it was not hot. It was really the best time of the year. Most parts of the country are about 6,000 feet above sea level. The winters were very cold, because there were no electric heating systems or firewood to make heat. So in winter it was very, very cold in the prisons. I felt the cold in my bones and remained cold all the time. The prisoners faced a lot of difficulties. When I had chains on my hands and feet, part of the iron bands that touched my body became a little bit warmer, but the rest of the chains were very cold. When they touched the body it felt like ice. So the winters in prison were very difficult.

Often in prison the devil would tempt me with thoughts like: You had a chance to leave during the jailbreak, why did you not take advantage of that? When I was discouraged, the Word of God would show me that God would not put me in situations beyond what I could bear. So when discouragements came to my heart, I simply prayed: "Lord, you know my mind and the discouraging thoughts that come, but your Word says that you will not put me in a situation beyond what I can bear. I thank you that you know I can bear it." Knowing that the Lord would not put me in a situation beyond what I could bear gave me courage and strengthened me in my circumstances.

Release from First Imprisonment

The government found it hard to keep me in prison, because many were becoming Christians. Before I was released, God spoke to me: Prem, go around the world and tell the people what I have done for you. I asked the Lord how I could go since I was in prison and still had more than a year's stay in prison to complete my six-year sentence. Then a voice told me again, "I say go."

I thanked the Lord and started to pray. "Lord, you have done so many things for me. If you send me into the world, what would be the one message to tell the people?" So I prayed that the Lord would give me one definite message for all the people. One night as I was praying in my room, there was a very powerful light. The room where

I was kept (with twelve other men) had no windows and only one door. There was no way that the light could come in. It was very dark. I opened my eyes and looked to the light. It was in one place, and it spread and spread all over one side of the wall. In that light, another powerful light moved across and wrote these words: "Preach this only." And a hand pointed out to the Cross. I was very happy that God had answered my prayer in a very visible way. I praised Him and thanked Him.

I started to think about what specific message of the Cross that God wanted me to tell others. Everyone knows about the Cross. As I meditated on that, I found that Jesus, on the Cross, made us all one through His blood. He purchased us on the Cross with the price of His own blood and made all believers in the world one body. It is a united body. So wherever I go, I try to tell people that Jesus made us one in His cross when we became Christians. No matter which part of the world we may have been born in and whatever our nationality, the day we accepted Christ we became a member of His body through the blood of Him who cleansed us.

One night God spoke to me again, "Prem, you will be released ninety days from now."

I told the Lord that I had more than a year's stay left in prison. The Lord spoke again, "I said you will be released in ninety days." I replied, "Thank you Lord." The next morning I asked for a calendar and counted the ninety days from that day and marked the date. I started telling people in prison when they became Christians that I would be released on that date and that they must continue the work. The ninety days passed very quickly and the day arrived when I expected to be released.

I gave my cooking utensils, blankets and extra clothes to others who had none. I dressed myself and prepared to go. However, up till twelve noon that day, nothing happened. Other prisoners (especially those who were communists) started to mock me and said there was no God. They told me to take my cooking utensils and clothes back so that I could remain in prison with them.

While they were talking to me, some people from the jail office came and said, "Call Prem Pradhan: he is released."

I said to those who had become Christians in that prison, "Brothers, they are calling me and I have to go. Let us pray." I prayed, and those who mocked me said that the prison authorities were just joking. I went to the gate and the police opened the first gate for me to go through. I waved my hand to say good-bye. The communists and other unbelieving prisoners said that I had great willpower. I told them, "I have a great God who never fails me."

Then the police opened the second gate and took me to the jail office. The jailer looked at me and said that the government had decided to release me. I had made more people Christian in prison than outside, so they gave orders to kick me out.

I told them that I had already known I would be released on that day. The jailer asked me how I knew, because the authorities had made a decision to release me only three days ago. I replied that I had known of my release three months ago and everyone in the prison knew about it. The jailer said that it was impossible, because it was a top secret. I told them that it may be a top secret for them, but for God this was decided three months before they told me. Then I was released.

The moving from one prison to another during the years of my imprisonment helped me to convert many. The tribes lived in different parts of the country. There were two large tribes. One was called Rai, and the other was called Nimbu. Whenever I was moved to another place, I was among a different tribe. That helped me to bring in new converts, and when they were released, they were sent back to their own tribes. In this way the church grew. That is how every tribe had their own "missionaries" to work with them.

4

Spread of the Gospel after Release from Prison

Upon my release, in 1965, I started visiting the churches again and found that wonderful things had happened. Jesus said, "I will build my church and the gates of hell will not prevail against it." The church had grown to about 5,000 people, and in some places there were groups numbering twenty, thirty, or fifty people.

At that time, I chose some brothers from each group, those who were preaching the gospel and winning souls boldly. For those who were called, I told them why they were called and why God had given them wisdom to do that work. I prayed before choosing those brothers; then I kept them with me, trained them, and sent them back to teach the people.

I was able to continue the work from 1965 to 1971. Sometimes I went to the churches and ordained elders and responsible brothers. All the elders of the church were not ordained at the same time because they had to prove their ability to lead the people, preach the gospel and handle the problems in the church that might arise due to persecutions. Those who handled these things well were recognized by the others within that group in the village. The group would suggest that this brother could be their elder. When I also felt the same way about that brother, I would lay my hands on him. I prayed and asked God to bless him that he might fulfill the will of God for him to be an elder.

Not all of the elders were able to read. An elder might have been a Christian for two, three, or seven years.

After the church was established in one village, I started to work again in another new place.

I began planting new churches in the same way that I had done before, but where there were no Christians. These places were in the extreme north and all over the mountains. The Lord helped me even more than before. I had learned so much in prison and I was closer to the Lord and He with me.

The Lord helped me to do a lot more work in healing the sick and raising the dead. Many became Christians. Also, I had learned in prison to choose brothers and train them. Then I sent them back to their own tribes.

Preparation of Workers

When I trained men, I took them with me on my travels. They saw with their own eyes how God healed the sick. I told them to pray, they did, and some people were healed. Then I would send them out, each taking a new Christian with him. Now I have ten men with me all the time.

This is what I mean by "Bible school training."

I was asked by a brother how I ran a Bible school in Nepal, since it was against the law. I told him that this Bible school had no signboard. Those being trained did not study to see how many chapters and books there were in the Old Testament. The training in my Bible school lasted for three months. During that time, Christians learned that they had to suffer and that even though they might have many difficulties, they had Jesus. I would share with them my experiences and also those of other brothers who were elders. If they could read, they read their own books and prayed. After three months, they would be sent out to preach the gospel. If they established a church, they did not come back again; they were to remain in that place and help the church to grow.

The workers were sent out in twos to each place. I never send them out alone, so if one has any trouble, the other can help. In the beginning, I went out alone because

I had no one to go with me; but still, I was not alone because Jesus was with me.

I tried to prepare people who could take my place. I know I have to leave this body and be with the Lord, so the Lord has to prepare people to take care of this work. Jesus said that the student and the teacher can be equal in the work, but the student cannot be above the teacher. The men I train copy what they see in me. If I am a bad example, then they will never be able to grow; so I have to walk fearfully before God in the way I live. What I teach I must practice; otherwise, people will not follow me. I learn from the Lord Himself, and I tell people that they can try to do the same as I do. Some are very good brothers, and they can take the responsibility of the work of so many Christians and so many churches.

Persecution Outside of Prison

To train workers, I took Christians who could read and write to travel with me, so then I did not travel alone. First I chose twelve men who stayed with me, and we traveled as a group. I took men from each tribe. When they were trained, I would send two of them to their own tribe. They preached the gospel, but it was not easy. During all those six years after my release from prison, the workers traveled with me, but it was not without many difficulties.

In one village, the other workers and I were hung from trees with our hands bound behind our backs. The leaders of the village took off our clothes and put brown sugar on our bodies so that flies and ants would bite us. It was difficult when we were bitten. With all the other brothers with me, I had to be more courageous. Because the leaders of the village knew that I was training these men, they gave me the most trouble. It was really painful, but because I faithfully suffered, these men also were able to suffer.

In one place, we were kept that way for seven days. We were treated that way by the leaders of the village because when Buddhists became Christians, then the Buddhist priests lost income. When they lost their income, they would turn very much against the Christians. That is why they persecuted us so much. However, in that same village today, there are 5,000 Christians. Only four Buddhist priests remained as unbelievers. The whole village turned and became Christian after we suffered.

At that time, there were seven families in the village who became Christians. (Two other men who became Christians were not yet baptized and did not face persecution like the rest.) The seven men were sent out of their homes, along with their families. They lost their cattle, their farms, their homes and everything. They were compelled to leave their village after the persecution. All the families moved to my farm where we stayed together.

I never stayed alone with just my family and children. There were always many Christians with us and we lived together. There are more than four hundred of us who live together. This farm is about twenty-five miles from the Indian border.

After the seven families had stayed on my farm for some time, we prayed and sought the Lord for direction. Wherever the Lord showed us, we sent each family to a different area. In every place where these families settled, there are now big churches. By this I mean that even though Christians may worship separately in smaller groups because of the distance between them, they are one body. In a whole area there may be more than four or five hundred people. All the seven brothers who left their village became evangelists.

The two Christians who remained secretly in the village that persecuted us were afraid to pray together. They came and asked us to pray for members of their family. I advised them to go back to their village and not to worry. They were to hide and not do anything openly. We would visit them secretly and pray with them in the forest. Our Christians would go out at night and pray for these believers and then come back. These two who remained Christians secretly spent many nights in the forest to pray, and God gave them strength. We had fellowship in this way.

Sometimes I visited a village and spent the night there. Nobody other than the believers would see me or know that I had visited their village. Christians went secretly to encourage people in villages. When people saw miraculous things like healings, and they saw that Christians were willing to hide a whole day or night in the forest so as to visit them secretly to encourage them and bring them food, they were moved, and they accepted Jesus.

Outside the prison, we were not exempt from suffering. I faced dangers from mobs. The Buddhist and Hindu priests in the village would stir up the people to start a riot. The mobs have killed Christians by poisoning their food or pushing them over a cliff in the mountains. If the bodies were found, the death was attributed to an accidental fall. There was continual suffering, all the time.

In prison there was no need to work and there was not much trouble physically, except for the chains and the food. But outside the prison, there were more difficulties. In our travels, there were not many shops in the villages where we could buy food. Sometimes we had to go without food or water.

Believer's Baptism and the Consequences of the Law

I do not baptize new believers immediately, but wait at least two years. When the converts grow in number and are prepared to suffer a year's imprisonment, then I take them down to the river and baptize them.

After baptism, the church is established openly and starts to grow. We do it this way because, until and unless people are trained and learn to suffer, they may not be able to face the difficulties of being cut off from their families. This separation usually happens after baptism. The government endorses this practice of disinheriting Christians.

I do not believe that baptism saves any man. A person is saved when he accepts Jesus. However, the government and the people believe that when a person gets baptized he cuts himself off from the whole family. The government also believes in sending the person who baptizes others to prison for six years. Anyone who is caught preaching will face a three-year imprisonment.

In doing the work, God gave us the wisdom to see that sometimes the pressure was too much. There was no need for people to do something which would cause more trouble; so when the pressure in a situation was high, we avoided activities that would draw attention to Christians. We stopped all baptism, kept quiet, and prayed in the forest or in the river- bed, but not in a home. Once the pressure subsided, we would start baptizing again and doing other things. Once believers were baptized, a fellowship of Christians was established in a home. The people in the village were then surprised to see that so many people had become Christians.

After I was released from my first imprisonment, I had a period of time (about six years) to establish more churches. Over and over again, the church grew. When I was sent to prison for the first time, there were about fifty Christians; but before I was sent to prison the second time, the church had grown to about 15,000 believers.

Follow-Up of New Believers

When someone becomes a Christian, we get all the elders in the new believer's church to follow up the new convert and encourage him. A new believer can give witness and tell the people he is a Christian the day or the week after he becomes a Christian. There are no rules about that.

When the elders observed that a brother was very zealous and did good work for the Lord, then they would come and tell me about him. So the elders watched and encouraged a new believer that showed potential; then they would bring him to the farm to stay there for a period of time.

All men have a different nature. This is why we cannot have any set rules. Some have a very bold nature and they do everything zealously, and others are more gentle. It does not mean that the brother who is gentle is a weak Christian and the bold brother is a strong Christian. Some brothers are gentle because that is their nature; likewise, some are bold because of their nature, too. Some men are gentle sometimes, but when they are put in difficult situations they can be very strong. They may look soft, but when trouble comes, they are the strongest in the group. And the seemingly strongest brother is often weak. On the other hand, sometimes the strongest brother is strongest and the weakest brother is weakest. There is no way to tell. And sometimes a brother may be strong for a long, long time and then become weak . . . and not only weak, but a stumbling block.

Regarding Men Who Have Been Called

I have always taught that every man who becomes a Christian is responsible to win others, so everyone has a call to preach the gospel. By doing such work, some would grow faster and win more souls than others did. When the elders and I saw this evidence in a man's life, then we would pray for him. We asked the Lord to enable him to give more time to God's work. Then we would try to help him with some money to go and preach the gospel.

When the church gathered together and worked together, everyone could discern that a certain brother had the call of God on his life, so they would encourage him. If he felt the same way, we would tell him to pray about his calling. We would tell him that we observed something in his work and that he could be used in a better way to preach the gospel to others. We reaffirmed the calling of God on these men's lives and have asked them to step out boldly. There were not many such men, but if a brother felt the same way we felt about him, he would come and tell the other elders, who would pray for him.

Growth and Development of the Church in Katmandu and Other Areas

Before I was sent to my first imprisonment, there were only fifty-four Christians. Some of these Christians worked in the hospitals that were started by the missionaries of the United Mission of Nepal. Some other brothers were brought over by the missionaries from India to work as pastors for the mission churches.

After my release from my first imprisonment, I did not try to bring the Christians back with me, because believers that were converted through my ministry were threatened with the loss of their jobs if they came to fellowship in my home. Those who worked in the hospitals were earning an income to support their families, and I did not want them to lose that.

I started to preach the gospel-meaning that I told people one by one about the Lord. When the people saw the healing and all that went on, they turned to the Lord, and I baptized them. Soon I had a good group of about fifty people who met in my home.

Those Christians who were converted through me and who worked in the hospital did not want to leave me. They wanted to have fellowship with my group because they received spiritual food and fellowship. At that time, the organized church had services on Sundays. In Nepal, Saturday is a holiday and Sunday is a working day. I prayed about this matter and I changed the meetings from Sunday to Saturday so that all could come to worship in my home. On Sunday they could go to the mission churches.

Today in Nepal, all Christians worship on Saturday because it is a government holiday. Among the people who became Christians, many were civil servants. They were schoolteachers, police, army officers and so on. It was difficult for them to come on Sunday since it was a working day. Therefore, we have continued to worship on Saturday. This was only in the capital city.

When there was a good group of Christians established in the capital city, I left the work in the hands of other brothers. I went into the mountains where there were no Christians. During that time, there were not many trained brothers available, so I traveled alone. Those brothers who were prepared in the capital city needed to stay and establish more churches there. They also did pioneer work, even in the city, starting churches in places where there were none.

I went to do pioneer work in the villages that were four or five days walk from the capital city. As I stayed there and started to pray and work, the Lord helped me. At first, in one place, only two families became Christian. I stayed with them and started the work. Slowly it grew into a group of people. Then the village Christians faced much trouble because of the Buddhist beliefs of the village.

In that village, the mother of a Christian man died. We gave her a Christian burial and did not call the Buddhist priest to have a ceremony. This brought much objection from the villagers and angered the priests. This was the place where all the Christian brothers and I were tied to a tree and kept that way for seven days. They told me that I must leave the village. The village head (who was elected by the government) decided that all of us must leave the village.

When the seven families moved to my farm, we had so many people who needed food, we decided to clear the land and make it into an agricultural farm. These families stayed with me on the farm and the Lord helped us. Later, after much prayer, we sent all the seven families to different areas, one by one. They did not all leave at the same time.

Establishment of Churches in New Settlements

In Nepal, as the population in the mountains grew, the people from the mountains came down into the valley. They settled in the lowlands that were unpopulated. These lowlands were government land and close to the forest. No payment was required because the government was encouraging new settlements to be started. The people only needed to pay the tax on the land, and the property became theirs for future generations. During that time, many people from the mountains came and settled on the government land. All the seven families who lived on my farm moved to settlements like these in different areas.

When one of the seven Christian families moved to a new settlement, we built a house for them and helped them with food. The rest who stayed behind would visit them. In that way the work started among the new settlers. Some settlers became Christians when we talked to them and prayed for the sick, so a new group of Christians was established.

In a new settlement, the people came from many areas. They had family and relatives in the mountain vil-

lages where they had lived before. After they became
Christians and went home on visits to their relatives, they
would talk to them about Jesus and pray for the sick. So
the gospel was spread further and further. This is one way
the church grew.

All of the six families who remained on my farm were
settled in different areas. They did the work of spreading
the gospel.

The new settlements that sprang up everywhere
helped us to cover many areas with the gospel. This does
not mean that we did not have persecution. We faced it
all the time.

Persecution of Christians in the New Settlements

In these new settlements the people were mostly Buddhists and some were Hindus. When the people turned to
Christ and were no longer following their customs and
traditions, then difficulties arose.

Everywhere, the priests received a portion of the crops
that were grown by the villagers. In ceremonies for the
newborn or for the dead, something was given to the
priests in the temples. The priests also received something
for the service of their sacrifices and prayers on behalf of
the sick. But when people became Christians, they no

longer practiced these traditions, and the priests were deprived of their privileges. So they stirred up the people to bring opposition. Sometimes it was reported to the government. With the law forbidding the change of religion, the government could take action, so people were arrested and made to suffer.

When settlers moved onto government land, they received temporary papers for the possession of their land. They did not have complete possession of it. Only after ten years would they receive legal papers for their land. Then the people paid taxes on the land. Sometimes the government took away the land from those who had been converted, and the people lost their land. After putting ten years of labor on their land, they did not have possession of it. This often happened to the elders of the church or to those who preached. They were the prime victims of punishment. The people reported against them since they were the ones who told others about Jesus.

Those who did evangelistic work were given much trouble and difficulties; and when a family lost their land, they came back to my farm. We prayed and sometimes God would help us to buy a little land in the same area that was not owned by the government. If God showed us to go to another area, then we would send these families to other areas. In that way, the church grew because of the many new settlements.

The government was upset that Christians were increasing so rapidly. The government insisted that Christian work must be stopped, because Nepal is the only Hindu kingdom in the world. Therefore, persecution was now more severe because the government was learning how easily people were converted. They tried to break the Christians and destroy the fellowship between the families that taught Christians and helped them to grow. Christians were put in prison and much pressure was being put on the older Christians. Still, the Lord's work kept on increasing.

The government began its own program of settlement for the protection of its natural environment. Many settlers had cut down too many trees and were destroying the forests. To put an end to this, the area was reclaimed and fenced in as government property, and the people lost everything again.

That became one of the hardest times for the church. The people were resettled on dry river beds which were mostly sandy land. The top soil had been washed away. The people faced many difficulties, because they had family and children to feed. I felt for the Christians who struggled, and I tried to help them from my farm. I gave them a water buffalo or a small piece of land if they had none. The Christians tried to work together on whatever land they had, to make it good for farming. In that way the work was done faster.

Where the Christians were settled by the government, they received an acre each. They all worked together (man, woman and child) to clear it quickly and transform it into farm land. When one family was settled into their land, then they would go on to the next acre of land and do the same thing all over again to help another family. So, the Christians settled faster than all the other settlers.

As other settlers saw how the Christians worked together, sang and prayed together, and healed the sick, they were won over more quickly to the Lord. That is how the church increased rapidly. Not only did the new settlers see that people were healed, but they also witnessed the practical ways the Christians helped each other. Non-Christians saw how the Christians were like one family, and it helped very much to promote the gospel. The rapid increase of Christians in Nepal was, in a sense, helped by the government's resettlement program. This fostered Christians to live close together in community, helping one another.

Establishment of Locations for Christian Gatherings

There are about 15,000 believers and sixty-five places where Christians gather to worship. These places are scattered in about thirty towns and villages. In some places a brother might be the leader of the group in his own home. If his home was big, the group met in his home. If another brother had a bigger home, the Christians would meet in theirs. Christians met in a home for worship.

The group that met for worship might not be made up of people from the same place. There might be just two or three families from the village where Christians gathered to worship. Another two or three families might be from another village that was two or three hours' walk away. Still others might live four or five hours away, coming from all directions.

The Christians would meet in a place where about twenty to twenty-five people were gathered together. When the group increased and there was no room to accommodate all in the same home, then we would ask some Christians to choose a home in another area where they could meet together. So, if there were five families from that same area, they could start gathering together, and another place for worship was established. If the number of Christians increased in one village where they were gathering, some could go to another place.

The Orphanage and School

The orphanage was started during my first imprisonment. It was not very big then. When I was sent to prison,

I had a son and a daughter. After I was released, I found that there were twelve children in my home. At first I was upset to find so many children in my home until my wife told me that these children were orphans. The law said that no one could change his religion; but if we took these children into our home and raised them in the Christian way, they would not be put in prison. I agreed with that and helped the children, along with the work I was doing.

Gradually, the children in my home increased to three hundred. Many of them are married now and have their own homes. Some are in Christian work, some are teachers, and others are in government service. The boys and girls that came then are all married and gone, but today there are still three hundred children in my home.

It is difficult for the western mind to understand that this is not a typical orphanage. The difference is that in my home these children have a father and a mother. I am the father and my wife is the mother. Even after the children have grown up and are married and gone, they return with their children once or twice a year to visit us. In the custom of my country, it is not unusual for a daughter who is married to return to her parents' home when the time for the delivery of her child is near. So, too, my "children" come home to us. It is home to them, not an orphanage.

In an orphanage, the children receive food, clothes, education and so on. But what they really need is the love of a father and a mother. Those that are brought up in the way of an orphanage do not have the love of anyone.

Although I was in prison most of the time, my wife and other Christian brothers looked after the children. Someone was there in our home acting as uncles and caring for the children; however, no one was the father. Only I am the father. When my own son and daughter were growing up, they called me Father, so all the adopted children called me their father too. I was father for all. Now my daughter has her own children and they call me Grandfather. Likewise, in the last three or four years, the other young children have also started to call me Grandfather because they hear my grandchildren call me that. So now, the children have a grandfather instead of a father; but they still call my wife Mother.

Today, even those that have grown up still call me Father. Once, I went to India to visit a sick man and was given a place to stay in a hotel. Two boys came and called me Father. I looked at them as they took my suitcase and things. I asked them where they were from. They replied that they were from Nepal. I told them that I did not remember where I had met them. They replied, "Oh, we were from your school, Father!"

Even the children in the school call me Father...all 1,200 of them! To them I am always Father.

Before finishing high school, most of the young people were baptized. Some went through Bible training, others looked for a job. If they were very good students, I would send them to college for education degrees so they could come back to work in my school. There is a need for more Christian teachers there.

At present, there are still 1,200 students in my school, which ranges from kindergarten to high school level, with a staff of 26 teachers. We do not receive any aid from the government because it is a private school, but we keep the same educational standards and requirements as the government schools. After the third grade, the government supplies the text books free. Of the 1,200 students, 300 of them are the orphans who live in my home.

So, all together, I had the high school on my farm and primary schools in four other places where there were many Christians. Not all the children who have grown up and left are Christians. Among the 26 teachers in my school, not all are Christians; but those who are live on my land. We also have 86 full-time native missionaries working in Nepal.

Growth of the Church from Education of Children

Many of the children that have grown up on the farm have their own families and children. This is one way the church increases. I do not count them unless believers are baptized and make a decision to follow the Lord.

Even the little ones in my home are growing up. They pray daily and they see how I live, how I love them and provide for them. So when they grow up and leave, most of them become Christians.

Those who are good students I send to college for further education. The rest of them who are willing, I train in the Bible school and then send them out. These are "missionaries" that have been prepared from the time they were children.

Establishment of Schools in the Rural Areas

In visiting the churches in different villages, I found that there was no work being done with the children who were from the Christian families. These children were innocently picking up the religious customs and traditions as they played with other children from families who were non-Christians. So I prayed, "Lord, I have made people Christians, but their children are worshipping and playing with other non-Christians. How am I able to bring them back to You?"

For the sake of these children, I started a school in the open field. For many years there was no building. It began small, from first to fifth grade. Gradually I increased its level, and the Christian children from the surrounding country villages would come to my school. Now the church had increased so much that I was not able to bring all the children into my home to educate them. Already I had a school of 1,200 children, with 300 who came from different areas where there were no schools. It was very hard for me to maintain it, providing food, clothing, books and everything for the children.

So, I started a new plan. When I would find twenty or thirty Christian families in one area, I would start a primary school for them, because there were so many Christian children. I built a thatched house as the school building. When the boys finished high school on my farm, they would be trained for evangelistic work first, and then they were sent as teachers to start a family school in the new settlements where there were Christians.

In the beginning, these schools were not in buildings. We helped the teachers who worked there with money to buy food. It took time before the government gave its approval to the school. The government now gives more help because it wants to improve education in the country. When a school applied for recommendation, they had to have at least fifty students. Then the government would sanction the school and give approval of the education. A thatched house had to be built as a school for the primary one, up to the third grade.

Today the government pays for some of the expenses after the third grade, such as books. In places where the schools have levels up to the fifth grade, the government pays the salaries of the teachers (including those that have been sent out from my high school). When the teacher is paid by the government, then the burden of the church to support the teacher is relieved.

Later, non-Christian children also came to these schools, so the teachers that I trained and sent out were able to convert the parents.

A brother who had received missionary training and who was zealous to convert others was sent out to teach the Christian and non-Christian children in the village school. In the evening he visited the homes of children from non-Christian families. When he had won the respect of the parents of these children, then he could share Christ with them. The teacher was respected in the village, and this facilitated contacts with parents. When they became Christians, they were added to the church, so the church increased.

5

Prem's Second and Third Imprisonments

It was while I was back visiting the eastern part of Nepal that I was arrested and put in prison for three years, beginning from 1971.

During the second imprisonment, I was put in another part of the country. While I remained in prison, I continued to do my work, telling people about Jesus. Prisoners became Christians and I was moved to another prison. I was kept moving from one prison to another as prisoners in each place became Christians. This helped me to bring other tribes to the Lord as prisoners were converted.

Release from the Second Imprisonment

After three years I was released. The native churches in Nepal had grown and increased, numbering about

15,000. They had not suffered loss. They continued to work faithfully and kept their faith. Sometimes they came to visit me and help me in prison, as I did my work there until I was released after I completed my three years' imprisonment.

I found, however, that my school in the capital city was closed by the government, and some of the Christians in the church there in Katmandu were taken over by the missionaries from the United Mission to Nepal. Not many Nepali Christians were won over by the Mission because of the persecution going on in Katmandu at that time. Many people were put in prison, including the teachers from the school and the missionaries, so Christians were afraid to worship at the school publicly and chose to meet in homes. At that time, the persecution of Christians occurred mainly in Katmandu.

When I was released, I spent my time visiting churches and concentrated on working on my farm so as to keep a low profile, because the government was keeping an eye on me. The brothers came to visit me on the farm, and in the evenings they came to my home. So I stayed on my farm and worked among the people, training and sending them out. That is the way I worked for awhile.

After two months, when I sensed that the government was no longer watching me so closely, then I started my work again. I told the other brothers to do the same thing:

that when there was much pressure from the government, they should just pray and remain quiet. But when the pressure was off, they could go out and work again.

At this time, the people who became Christians were mostly from the eastern part of Nepal. I visited them more often, because the church in the western part of Nepal was well-grounded and had good brothers to look after it. I would work in areas where there were few or no churches.

From 1974 to 1978, the churches in the eastern side of Nepal grew and increased. We had a good number of people. The churches on the western side of Nepal increased even much more, because new settlers were coming from different areas and were being reached.

Prem Pradhan's Third Imprisonment

Once again the government arrested me and sent me to prison because I converted many to Christ in the eastern part of Nepal. This time I was sentenced to prison for sixty years. It was in December of 1977.

I was sent to the prison in the capital, where political prisoners were kept. I was sent there because the authorities thought that these prisoners might not convert. But there also the Lord helped me, and many of them became Christians. When the authorities found that out, they sent me to the place where the mentally sick were kept.

In Nepal there was no hospital for crazy people. The mentally sick were put in prison and I was thrown in with them. Since these were crazy people, the door of that prison was left open. There was no need to lock them in. Because the room was very dirty, I would sit outside the door of the room with my coat on. That is the way I slept, just sitting there.

One night a voice told me to leave the spot where I was sitting. It was a difficult thing for me to do, because it was the one place where I could sit. All the other places in that room were filthy. I took my box, went a little further to another corner and sat there. A man came and sat down at the same spot that I had just vacated. After a few minutes, another man came and was searching for something. He found a big stone and came up to the man who was sitting where I had sat before and hit him on the head. Then he drank the blood. He would keep hitting the man on the head in different areas and licked the blood from his head. I went to the guard and told him that there was a mad man killing another mad man with a stone. The guard sent out an alarm and many other guards came. They saw the man who was still drinking the blood of the other. He became very strong and furious, and it was very difficult to drag him away from the bleeding body. It took four or five guards to take him out of the prison. He was put in an iron cage in the prison of the capital city. Only very crazy and dangerous men were put there. I thank God that a voice told me to move and to sit in another place. Had I sat and slept outside the door of that room, I would have been dead. Another man died in my place, and I escaped death.

I stayed in prison with the mentally ill for awhile longer. Then the jailer and others transferred me back to another part of the same prison where the normal prisoners were kept.

They had put me with the people who were mentally ill, in the hope of trying to get me killed. But the Lord helped me to stay alive.

Even among the crazy and mentally ill people, there were many who were healed.

Jesus told us to cast out demons. During my stay with the mentally ill people, I prayed for them and many were healed.

Back with the regular prisoners, I started to work among them again. I tried to do more work, because I knew this time I would never be released. I was given a sentence of sixty years in prison or the alternative of finishing a one-year imprisonment with payment of a heavy fine. This fine came up to a large sum of money.

At that time the Nepali Christians tried to get money for my release. The total sum needed was $20,000. Many of the Christians sold their gold and whatever they had, trying their best to raise that money. It was a lot of money for rural Nepali people.

In some way, I did not know how, a brother by the name of Bob Finley came to Delhi and found out that I was in prison again. He was told that I had completed a year of my sixty-year sentence and that the church in Nepal was trying to raise money to get me out. After that, some money was sent to the brethren in Nepal. The full amount was paid for my release.

During my third imprisonment, one brother wrote to other brothers in the church in Nepal. He stated that I would not be able to return to them again because I had a sentence of sixty years. He also said the Lord had shown him that he was chosen to continue the work in my place. He started his own work and took some of the brothers with him. The rest were preoccupied with raising the money for my release. When I was released from prison, the brother who had taken my place said that he tried to do the work because he felt that I would not be able to come back again. Still, he continued to do his work separately, but he was not able to hurt the church.

Today, he has given up the work and no longer wants to keep the people separate from us because he is tired. He wanted to bring the people back to my fellowship, but I told him that in the capital city there were many Christians already and that there was no place to keep them. It would be better for him to have the Christians meet in his own home. I told him that I could send others to join him in his home if he would not change the pattern of the church in Nepal.

How God Used Imprisonments for the Furtherance of the Gospel

When I was put in prison three different times, many people said that the devil did it. I do not believe that. It was God who sent me to prison because I was able to reach more new tribes in prison. I could not have managed it if I had had to do all that walking in the mountains. It would have been impossible to go from tribe to tribe to reach all the people that I reached through the prisoners from the various tribes. When the government transferred me from one prison to another, I was placed in the area of another tribe. It was an easier way of winning different tribes to the Lord.

That is why I believe God placed me in prison; for establishing churches and for His glory.

Today people who serve the Lord make their own plans. They decide where they will go to do evangelistic work, and they spend much money to put up all kinds of programs. Then they set up mission boards to plan all kinds of budgets, and they ask God to bless their work and confirm it. These people want the confirmation from God-that He might do the work according to their will. They forget that He has all power in heaven. He is the almighty God and He has His own plan.

God only needs men who are willing to suffer and work according to His own will-God's will. That is what is needed. When I travel in the West, I find it hard to tell and teach these things to people. They always want to preach God but not to obey Him. Rather, they expect God to obey them. That is the difficulty today in God's work.

6

Characteristics of the Church in Nepal

Church Government

In Jerusalem, when Christians were increasing rapidly and things were not working properly, the apostles agreed to choose seven men and gave them to the work of service. I did not find anywhere that the church had an election.

Sometimes one or two brothers who disagreed with the majority might find that they had been wrong and would come to agree with the rest of the group. At other times the majority might find that the one or two brothers who disagreed were right in their judgment all along. There is no democracy of votes or election in our church.

Church Elders

In Nepal, a local church may have two, three or four elders. Then there is a more experienced elder who helps

supervise, strengthen and encourage the other churches. He is in charge of the section of Nepal in which he lives. All together, there are seven elders over the seven sections outside the capital city. They help to look after the churches.

In addition to those seven elders, there are two other elders who preside over their local churches in the capital, Katmandu. The duty of these nine elders is to get the report from all the churches in Nepal, take care of financial matters and advise how the funds from tithes should be used, and so on. Altogether, the nine also make decisions regarding the purchase of land for church building. I would be present as a fellow elder, so there are ten men altogether.

Ministry to the Sick in Nepal

The men and women in the fellowships in Nepal pray for the sick. God heals through them as well as through me and the other workers. People bring their sick, and the Christians gather together to pray for them. It is not just one person who prays, but all together Christians pray for them. Everyone prays.

The Christians gather in the mornings now to pray. All the Christians kneel around the sick to pray for them. Sometimes healing comes very quickly; sometimes it takes

time. And not everyone is healed. People are not healed every time because we cannot command God to do anything. Whatever is His will He will do. Most of the time, God has healed, because the people who brought the sick came a long distance from their homes. The sick might be carried on makeshift stretchers, or if it was a young child he would be carried on an adult's back. Those who carried the sick might have walked a day or two to come to the place where Christians meet. The fact that these people traveled so far showed that they had faith to be healed, so God respected their faith and our prayers. Often the sick were brought to us after their gods had failed to heal them in their temples. God healed them.

In Nepal, people who are not Christians who are sick will naturally go to the temple, the priest or the witchdoctor. Here in the States, people who are sick will naturally go to their doctor for treatment.

Once, while in the States, my glasses were cracked in many places and I could not see properly. I went to an optical shop to try to change them. The people who worked there asked me for my prescription, which I did not have. I told them that I did not need to have my eyes tested since I only wanted some reading glasses. They refused to do it, so I thanked them and left. I would change my glasses when I returned to Nepal. Here in America, for a little thing like reading glasses, one needs a

prescription. How could people get courage to come to the Lord and be healed without a prescription?!

In America, a church may not be raised up on the basis of miracles of healing, as we can in Nepal. However, we can increase the faith of the people.

Work On the Farm

On the farm I have other Christian families who help me in the farming. These nine families live in different homes but in the same area on the farmland.

There is more work to do outside of the prison than there was when I was in. I have 300 acres of farm land and only two tractors to plow it. A lot of work is involved in sowing seeds and growing crops. In America, there is only one season for growing crops. In my country, we have two or three crops in one field. The work has to be done because I have to feed so many children. Also, all the Christians who are thrown out of their family or villages come to me because they need food.

Everyone has to help take care of the land. When I am not there, they have to keep on working. They work hard, but they need someone over them to look after things. The responsibilities of the farm are mine. When I asked these people to release me so that I could have my retirement just to pray and study, no one was willing to do

that. The people said that they would be willing to divide the work among them, but they wanted me to stay with them. That is one difficulty that I am facing presently.

Prem's Work in the Nepalese Community

I was made mayor of my village and had an office with eleven men to work with me. One of my duties was to collect land tax, but I left it to the men to do it. A poor country remains poor because most of the money that is collected goes into the pockets of corrupt officials and not for the betterment of the land. I did not want to be seen in that way, so I let others handle the money.

During the first five years as mayor, I helped to develop sites for drinking water and water canals for the irrigation of the land. I started a market, a school, and many other things. Half of the tax money that was collected went to the administrative center and the other half was used within the area. The money was used efficiently.

When my term expired, I no longer wished to continue in the post of mayor. The people, however, insisted that I be their mayor because they saw that their land and their lives had improved. I would much rather devote my time to reading, praying and converting people to Jesus Christ. That is a lot less work, and I completely forget what is going on in the outside world. However, I believe

that Jesus Christ is the builder of His church. He takes the responsibility of the work when I am not there. He raises some of the brothers to take responsibility. Because of the injury to my leg caused by my imprisonments, I am not able to do as much work as I would like, and I am not able to travel in the mountains now.

Taking the Lord's Supper

The first church was established when I baptized seven believers in a village. Then I went to their home and took the Lord's supper with them. I made the bread out of wheat flour. In our country there is no grape juice, so I boiled water and added sugar to it as a substitute for the wine.

I explained to these believers that the one bread represented the body of Christ. This body was not just the eight of us: There were many Christians in the world, and all of them have a part of this bread. We gave thanks, broke the bread and took a piece each. Then we all drank from the same cup. That was the way we had the communion service.

We always gave thanks to the Lord before we took part in the Lord's table. Every member of the body gave thanks to Jesus for saving his soul and for suffering for us at Calvary. If there was anything bad in their hearts before they took part in the Lord's table, they were to ask God for forgiveness. When we became Christians, our soul

was saved, but sometimes we still do wrong because we are in a human body. Everyone must judge his own heart and make confession if needed before he partakes of Christ's body.

These Christians gathered together on Sunday to break bread as I had shown them. They began to invite their relatives and friends to their homes, and the church was started in that way.

I stayed a few more days with the new group of believers to teach them. Before I left them to go to another place to preach the gospel and establish churches, I chose a man who could read, and I left him with the Gospel of John and told him how to conduct the service. On my way back, I visited these Christians again and found that they had invited their friends and relatives and prayed for them. So I talked to these people, and sometimes I baptized more new converts. When a small nucleus of Christians became a bigger group, I told them to choose a "responsible brother," one who would be responsible for the meetings.

Many people from the organized church have asked me, "Brother Prem, you were alone as the first Christian, and you founded the first church with those early converts. Who ordained you for the work of the ministry and baptizing people?" I quote them the verse from John's Gospel that said, "You have not chosen me but I have chosen you

and ordained you. Go and bring forth fruit." So I told them that my ordination was from the Word of God.

Special Meetings

Another service that I have is called the "laying-on-of- hands service." In this service I lay hands on believers and ask the Lord to fill them with the Holy Spirit.

In that meeting with those first seven believers, three of them spoke in tongues. I taught them, however, that just because the others did not speak in tongues, it did not mean that they were not Christians. We received the Holy Spirit when we believed, but the manifestation of the Holy Spirit in some might be that God had a special gift for them.

While I was with those believers, we met together every evening after the day's work to read the Gospel of John. I wrote down some of the songs I had learned from Brother Bakht Singh's assembly and taught them. Later on, they wrote their own songs to Nepali tunes.

Home Meetings

For the Sunday worship, the church meets at 10 a.m. All the Christians gather together. Some may come from far away, requiring a three- or four-hour walk. All the baptized believers come together to break bread.

When Christians gather together, they pray first, asking God to help them to worship Him, and they pray that evil powers will be stopped from disturbing the meeting. Sometimes the police or other people might come to disturb our meetings and arrest our people, so we always pray for protection, that we might have the freedom to worship. (This does not mean that we have to do this in every church or every meeting. Everyone prays as the Spirit of the Lord leads them.)

Then we sing songs, take communion, pray for the sick, and share a witness. Believers might testify to something that has happened-some sorrow or joy, whatever it may be-and they pray for one another. Those who are able to read the Bible might read certain passages from the New Testament. Then they share its practical application in the light of present circumstances.

Through the reading of the Word, believers encourage and exhort one another.

No one has "prepared messages" to preach from. Some brothers are good teachers and they will teach.

Note: While Prem Pradham was speaking these messages, Gene Edwards interjected some relative comments. You will be able to recognize these comments, as they are slightly indented.

Gene Edwards: Among the many things that Prem said the people did in their meetings, he said they gave their testimony. This will rob the pulpit of its position. If the nature of these meetings is watered and cultivated, it will take away the everlasting focus on sermons, which robs God's people of functioning and wreaks carnage on the body of Christ.

Apart from Sunday worship, we have prayer meetings daily. These meetings have no specific times when they start because a few Christians may be from the same village and others may live in another place one or two hours' walk away.

For instance, if a meeting was held in my home, I would return early from work. We would spread a few mattresses on the floor, and the few that arrived first would start to pray and sing. Another family might arrive, and eventually we might have four, five or six families gathered together. Those that traveled far would sleep in the home where the meeting was held. In some villages, there might be just two or three families.

During the planting season of wheat or corn, Christians might not be able to meet together at night because they had been working hard all day and were too tired. We might not meet for two or three days, and then we would come together again when we were able. There is no law

that says we have to do things in a certain way, because we all have the freedom of the spirit.

In Nepal, when a bear chases a man, he follows the footprints of the man. If the man turns two times around a tree, the bear will do the same and then continue chasing the man. So the bear runs after the man according to the man's goal and follows his footprints. A church cannot follow the footprints of man. We call that a "bear line."

Gene Edwards: It is our experience that the church is not just meetings. Out of the meeting comes a knitting together, a closeness and a love for one another. This grows not only in the meetings, but into a daily caring for one another-in the day time brothers working together, sisters going to one another's homes to take care of each other. That makes the church not a meeting, but a way of life. It is the daily living of your whole life. At times we quit meeting for weeks just to rest, but the church goes on. Church is a way of life. Without meetings, the life of the church is not even hampered at all. The experience of the brothers and sisters enjoying the Lord together continues. In so doing, we discover that church is not confined to a few hours, but it is our daily life. We need to get liberated from our routine. Even if we do not have a ritual from

day to day, if we get liberated from routine, then we have something that goes beyond anything we have understood about the church. Something becomes alive on earth. It becomes a living organism and a civilization within itself.

Baptism

Baptism is also another testimony. Non-Christians come to see the baptism when I baptize believers in the river. I remind believers that they are promising to follow Jesus and that God and his Holy Spirit and the angels are present to witness that event. Also the church, the body of Christ, is present. So too are the powers and the principalities. I tell the believer who is getting baptized that before all these witnesses, he is declaring that he has died with Christ, was buried and raised from the dead. From that day he is to live a new life and never, never deny Jesus. They promise that they will never deny Jesus.

Christian Funeral

A funeral service is another testimony for Christians. All the Christians gather in the home of the person who died.

The Hindus or the Buddhists bind the body of their dead, hang it with a rope, and take it to the place where it is burned. Then the people weep and mourn before it is burned. As Christians, we do it differently. We build a wooden coffin for the body, put flowers on it, and take it down to the river bed. Many people follow us to see how Christians bury their dead. The elders read from the Bible and testify that when Jesus comes to receive us, this dead brother will be raised. We who are alive will be transformed, and together we will be with the Lord. Instead of weeping, the Christians sing songs and give thanks that this brother is taken home and that they will see him again. We do not weep, because we have a sure hope. That brings joy to the family of the dead.

The non-Christian relatives who are present hear about the Christian's hope of the resurrection from the dead. The Christian burial is a good testimony for the non-Christians. That is the best time to preach the gospel. Many were brought to the Lord that way.

How Believers Help One Another in Nepal

The Christians in Nepal help one another. They prove to the non-Christians that they are one family. The church

might be made up of people from different tribes, but they become one family.

A few years ago there were no roads. Sometimes it took a few days' walk (as many as two to six days) just to go to a place to buy salt. If, for instance, there were seven Christian families in the village, then all the six brothers would go together to buy salt. One brother remained to look after all the families. The six brothers who went together to buy salt would carry extra for the brother who remained in the village.

One of the men had to remain in the village because the cattle needed to be sent to the forests for grazing. Every family might own some goats, sheep, cows and buffaloes. The brother who remained would supervise the older boys in the families to graze their animals in the same area. In that way Christians helped one another. The women in each of the families would take care of the children.

In the villages, people who have thatched-roof homes need repairs on their roof every two or three years. If a believer's home needed repairs, all the Christians would go to that home and the men would work on it together. Sometimes the work is completed in a day. In this way, the brother who received help would save money.

The church, as a corporate witness, had a greater impact on the non-Christians than the preaching of the

gospel itself. It is a wonderful thing to live as a family and care for one another. The sick would be taken care of. The elderly who were without families would be taken into some home. The church would help them and pray for them. If they died, they would be given a Christian burial.

How the Church Cares for Children

In Katmandu where the church meets (about 100 to 150 people now), there are many young children. Those under ten years of age would be taken care of by a sister who worked well with them. They would be kept on another side of the building where they could sing songs or play. If they were hungry they would be fed in the kitchen. The services might last two, three or four hours. There was no fixed time for the length of the meeting.

In the villages the children were handled differently. One of the brothers or a young mother would take the children outside. They could sing or play in the garden. The village children would also come to join them and learn Christian songs. In the wintertime when it was too cold for the children to be outside, they would be kept in another house. The young babies stayed with their mothers.

Young boys and girls who are thirteen or fourteen stayed at home to take care of the animals. In the homes in Nepal, the animals were kept on the ground floor and the family lived above it. During the Sunday service while the adults were gone, the older children would take the animals to the forests for grazing during the day and bring them back in the evening. Sometimes they might have the responsibility of caring for the animals of four or five families.

Church Finances

Whatever the believers in the village had, they gave a tenth to the church. If they grew crops or sold something, for example their animals, they would give a tenth of the money to the church. There was no system of collection or passing a collection plate around. The people brought their tithes to the place where these things were kept. After the meeting was over, the elder took care of those things.

Sometimes people walked a long way to come to a meeting (three or four hours' walk). They might have their food in the morning before they came. But when they left at 3 p.m to go home, it would be night time when they got home. For these families who walked a long way, the family in whose home the meeting was held

would cook for them. So these families would eat before they went on their journey home. The tithes were often used for such purposes.

Some Continuing Burdens of the Work in Nepal

Today in Nepal, 200 Christians are held in police custody. This means that the government will not supply them any food until they are imprisoned. Therefore, the families will have to supply the food. Even in prison, they are only given some rice and firewood to cook it.

It is a difficult time for the people, and that is why I must return, because they look to me for advice.

I have told my people, those who are Christians, to start setting aside a handful of rice from each meal and keep it. Then when they gather together, the host family should keep it for the elders to collect it. This collection is not only from the church in one place, but all over the country. Somebody has to bear the risk of taking food to the Christians who are in police custody. Police officers have sometimes arrested those who brought food for the Christians, when they discovered that these men were also Christians. Because of that, I advised those who brought food to the prison to identify themselves as relatives of the Christians. The Lord said we must be innocent as doves

but wiser than the serpent. So Christians must learn not to tell lies, but to avoid answers that might cause them to be imprisoned.

When both parents of a family are in prison, other Christians have to come and help look after their children and their animals. This is another task for the church, and is not an easy thing to do. Many Christians have to be sent distances to care for the children, the animals and the farms. People are not arrested in just one place, so Christians have to care for families in many places.

Also, many of the leading brothers of the churches are in hiding from place to place. Two or three weaker brothers are left to look after the church. Those who are in hiding face much difficulty, for they have no place to sleep or food to eat until they reach some Christian's home. We must pray much for them.

I have much peace now to return to Nepal, even though I may be arrested. I do not know what is happening in the churches, and I hope to travel as much as I can to encourage the brethren, in prison and outside. Pray for me, that the Lord will help me to encourage them and to build up their faith.

The church is not able to meet together right now, and they need your prayers. The Bible school has been closed, and the students have gone out to preach the

gospel. There is much work to be done looking after the pupils in the high school and hiring teachers. Pray that the Lord may help me to do all these things.

Also, my wife has to look after all the children. When I am gone, the whole burden of the many children and the farm falls on her shoulders, for all come to her for help. It is difficult for her to manage everything.

Financial Support of the Work in Nepal

In America it is hard to make Christians understand how God is raising up people to work in their own native land. However, as God is closing the door for foreign missionaries to go into other countries, people are slowly beginning to see how native workers are more effective in their own land than are missionaries.

Now, denominations are giving financial help to the native missionaries of Nepal. However, it puts a hook on them. The native workers have to follow the constitution or the pattern of the denomination that helps them financially. Those who do not want to work under the rules of a denomination (but seek to work in God's pattern and God's way) are not given help. No one wants to help me. If I worked as a Pentecostal or a Baptist, they would help me, but if I work as a Christian, no one wants to help. But

thank God, people are slowly beginning to understand and are changing their minds.

Individual Christians are now beginning to personally support the indigenous missionaries in different areas. Now we have more than forty full-time workers working in the headquarters and seven in Canada. God helped us in establishing our mission to help indigenous churches.

Some but not all the money for the buildings that were built on my farm came from the organization called Christian Aid. Some money came through my preaching. I never looked at how much money was sent to me. I simply did the work. Christian Aid might have provided half of the money that I received, and I brought in the other half by my farm which is now a very productive farm. It brings in between U.S. $40,000 to $45,000 a year. That farm has been most helpful in God's work. I did not know how much money was received nor did I see how much money came in for my work in Nepal. Whatever the amount sent was fine with me.

People in my country trust me. For instance, businessmen helped me by providing the building materials that I needed without requiring that I pay them first. In that way I could work and pay them little by little.

7

Effect of Missionaries on the Work in Nepal

There are no missionaries in Nepal, not officially. Those who are missionaries come into Nepal as medical doctors and educators. They are required to sign a statement saying that they will not preach the gospel nor make proselytes. By being in the country, they seek to establish a Christian presence.

When the nine Christians and I were thrown into prison, these missionaries were fully aware of the situation. Some of them wanted to identify themselves with our native church, but their mission boards would not allow it. For that reason, several left the country. Those who remained signed a written statement and sent it to the court saying that they would have nothing to do with the Nepali Christians: "We have not done any Christian work. Everything is done by Prem Pradhan. He is responsible. We have no connection with the churches in Nepal."

When I came out of prison, I found that the missionaries had taken over my work and had brought two brothers over to their side. These men were Nepalese but were citizens of Darjeeling, India. I knew them and they were very good brothers.

While I was in prison, the missionaries had asked me if these men could come from India and help in my work in Nepal, and I felt that it would be all right. (One of them became a Christian in the assembly of Brother Bakht Singh. Another brother was a Hindu convert from Darjeeling, India.) I had thought that it would be a wonderful idea to have these come and help the churches, but I did not know that they had been spoiled by the devil and by the missionaries. These men had left the assembly and were working with the missionaries. I did not know that brother R.C. had been sent to Bible school in England by the missionaries and had become part of the World Council of Churches. All this took place while I was in prison, and I was totally unaware of what went on; so when I was given their names, I was glad that the missionaries wanted to bring them over from India

These men took most of the Christians and the work of Nepal into their own hands, including the Nepal Christian Fellowship, which was a conference of our Christian workers. The Fellowship was started before I went to prison, and there was no membership or denomination.

It was not a church or an organization. That was why it was named the Nepal Christian Fellowship. But while I was in prison, those brothers came and made it into an organization.

After I was released, they invited me to preach in their meetings, in the same place where I was imprisoned. So I went. At that time there were no roads, and brother R.C. was in charge of those meetings. I stayed in his home because I had no home. I was just released from prison. In those meetings I delivered the message that God had given me—that there was one body. Those meetings lasted four days, and I taught especially from the Gospel of John (Chapters 14 to 17). All that time I taught them about the unity of the body and what Jesus' last prayer for the church meant.

Just after those meetings, the missionaries called a business meeting because they wanted to organize the Nepal Christian Fellowship in a certain way. While I was in prison, I had written a little constitution for the Fellowship because I had been asked to do so. Now the two brothers wanted to change it because the missionaries did not agree with it. Having joined the World Council of Churches, their opinions differed from my New Testament church constitution. I saw that the churches would not be free to follow the pattern of the New Testament church if they held to the opinions of the World Council

of Churches. I could not agree with the proposal for the changes to be made to the constitution of the Fellowship, so these brothers opposed me and withdrew my membership from the Nepal Christian Fellowship, although I was its founder. At that time they established a membership rule. I prayed about it and felt the Lord telling me to wait and see. So I waited several years.

Meanwhile, I continued in my work but did not force people to conform to my pattern. I did not want to force anyone to do anything if they did not agree with the way I felt. When the time came, I visited the churches; and within six months, I baptized another five thousand Christians.

As for those Christians who had gone to join the Mission, I did not request them to come back. Those who would not have anything to do with the Mission remained with me. I prepared more workers to be sent out to preach the gospel. First I would take twelve Christians with me, train them and send them out to the twelve tribal areas to preach the gospel in their own tribal language. The church started to grow and did not stop, in spite of the trouble that came from the organized churches and the missionaries.

The organized church tried their best to get me to join them as a bishop and to do all kinds of things. They promised that they would help me financially. When I rejected it, then all kinds of slanders were spread against me. I was accused of not keeping the unity among the churches and

of dividing the churches. In fact, it was the very opposite. I had always taught the people that there was one body. I never believed that there were two bodies. There is only one body of Jesus Christ. He is the head and we are the members of His body.

People who had not heard me speak did not know me. Many new missionary doctors and nurses came from overseas, and news was spread to them, and all over, that Prem Pradhan divided the church. People believed this slander because they did not know me. Once they met me or heard me speak, they would change their minds.

A doctor and his wife from Pennsylvania taped my message in one church and came to oppose me; but when they, being medical doctors, heard my preaching and saw with their own eyes that God was healing people (for a paralyzed woman was healed), they repented. They asked me to come to their home and have dinner with them. I went the next day. The doctor's wife wept and said, "Forgive me brother, for, not knowing you, I told bad things about you." I replied that I did not know whether she told good or bad things about me, for I did not hear them; but if she did tell it to someone, she should write to them and ask them to forgive her. The doctor was a rich man and wanted to help me financially, but I told him that I could not accept money from a man who did not know Jesus. Only God's money can be used for God's work, not the money of someone who was not a Christian. So I rejected the offer.

The Lord's work continued to grow in spite of all the slanders about me. I have been a Christian for more than thirty-eight years now. Of all those years, more than thirty-five of them have been spent in establishing the church in Nepal.

We have eighty-six full-time indigenous workers inside Nepal. They are establishing churches where there are no Christians. They are the real "missionaries."

My definition of a missionary is someone who is called out to establish churches. They are the evangelists and the church planters. Those who wanted to promote their own denomination could not understand this truth: that sending a man from one tribe to another was not profitable. The customs, culture and food differed from one tribe to the next, and outsiders only created a barrier instead of helping. Many did not agree with me. I had much trouble from missionaries because of this.

The Status of Foreign Missions in Nepal

During my first imprisonment, the foreign missionaries who were serving under the World Council of Churches made the declaration to the West that Christians in Nepal were suffering persecution, so they raised a large amount of money "for the Christians in Nepal," which numbered fifty people at that early time. This money never went into the hands of any of the Nepali brothers and sisters. Instead, it was used for the building of missionary hospitals and schools in Katmandu. Then the missionaries went to our Christians and offered them jobs in these institutions. All of this was a deliberate effort to take the Nepali Christians out of my hands. Also, they spread slander regarding me because I did not agree to join them.

The founders of the United Mission to Nepal, Dr. B. H. and Dr. and Mrs. M., were very wealthy people. Although they had never met me, much less known me, they spoke much against me. Dr. Frederick, who knew me before I was imprisoned, never spoke against me. He knew how I worked and what I taught. Later he visited me when I was in prison.

Those who spoke against me did so because I told the people that it was no use spending God's money to build hospitals and yet do nothing for the gospel. I have changed my mind since then, because I feel that my country needs medical help. We have only 445 doctors in the whole country.

There are many missions working now through India and Nepal-for example, Campus Crusade. They pay the indigenous missionaries who work for them. Some of them have also taken the men whom I have trained, to work for them. But I am happy now because my poor Christian brothers receive about $100 a month. These foreign missionaries may have their work and their churches, but they can never change what I have taught the Nepali Christians. That will always remain in their hearts.

Since the Nepali Christians receive money from foreign missions and organizations such as Campus Crusade, they might work according to the instructions of the mission; but these brothers have been trained by me and they have been with me for many years. So, when these foreign missions took our people and paid them to work, I sent them and told them to go and establish churches.

Never before have we, the church in Nepal, increased so much. The mission people would only remain in one church. They have not been able to establish their denomination, because they were using my people. The Nepali workers used the financial support given them to establish churches, but they remained faithful to the Word of God and to me. So, I have changed my plans now. Let the foreign missions send as much money as they can to Nepal to spread the work of the gospel. We will use it to spread the Word of God as it is written. I do not feel bad about this, because I have no money. Why not allow other people who have money to give to my brothers?

There was a man who, from the age he was in kindergarten, had been supported by me. I sent him to my high school and I trained him. He worked for three years, and his father was an elder. Another mission called Team Mission came into Nepal and built a hospital. I gave this man to be a pastor of their church, and he receives $150 a month. I am not worried about this because he was trained by me.

It is all right if the foreign missions take the workers that I have trained. Take my men, I will give them, but build the church!

The workers that I have trained may take on the name of the group they work for: Full Gospel, Campus Crusade, and so on; but they do not have a signboard to say so. As far as the work is concerned, these workers are doing the same work as I have done and are establishing churches in the same way.

I have changed my plans because I am not able to support all of my full-time workers. They number about eighty-six people, and I am still training more and more, sending them out to do the work. Also, whatever income I get from my farm goes to feed the children and to pay the teachers. I cannot keep up with all that. Let the foreign missions help, and the churches will grow more and more. We are 35,000 believers and are a strong group.

Those who work with Team Mission are different. Team Mission has a hospital in western Nepal that was started three years ago. They also have Nepali workers in the hospital. Some were converted through these people, but when trials came, they could not stand. Those who were trained by me, however, would go through trials and stand in truth. They will suffer persecution and not turn back because they were trained from the beginning to suffer.

There are two different types of Christians that are found in Nepal today. Some of the Nepali Christians who were converted in India are back in the country. They seek to work with foreigners and will have nothing to do with me. They have not been trained by me, and so I leave them alone. I try to pray for them. I send brothers to meet and to fellowship with them and to teach them the truth. If they see the truth, then I am happy.

These Nepali people that were converted in India by some mission board always try to find foreign missions to work with. I feel that they do not fully understand the truth. They are still nominal Christians and know little about Jesus or about suffering; so when suffering comes to them, they deny that they are Christians. I do not judge them, but I care for their souls, and that is why I send my people to meet them when they profess they are Christians. These nominal Christians often seek out foreign Christians and tourists because they hope to leave Nepal and come to America. I do not like this, but it really is a difficult thing when visitors have so much money, and

Nepal is open to tourists. These foreigners come and take one man and then another, and I cannot stop it.

There was a group called The Children of God who took a brother from me and he was spoiled by them. They came as tourists and took him. Very cunningly these foreign groups take our people, and those that are doing it now are worse than Campus Crusade.

For instance, Pocra is a big tourist center. It has a trekking center, a very beautiful lake and snow mountains. The village people bring their sheep and goats and other things to sell there. We prepared our Nepali Christian workers to reach them with the gospel because they are a northern tribe that comes from far away. When the tourists come to our country, they come to that place. So, knowing that our Nepali Christians now work in that area, the foreign missionaries came from other countries with the intention to make contact with our workers. It is a very good place to contact local workers.

Missionaries came as tourists and told our workers that they were also Christians. Our people had been taught that we are "only Christians." They were unaware of the many different groups in the West. So they would receive these foreign Christians into their homes and show them love and hospitality. But these Christians who came from outside of Nepal knew of me. They would not speak against me, but they would say that I have so much work to do that I would not have time to teach them everything that was in the Bible. Then, opening their Bibles and using verses of Scripture, they would try to convert the Nepali Christians to their thinking. When these foreign Christians left, they would give our Christians some money and the impression that they wanted to help them. When they came again the next time, to make further contact, they would make offers for our workers to work for their mission. Then they would also try to recruit others through the ones whom they hired to work for them. In that way some of our people are being taken.

If those groups were sound in their teaching, I did not say anything; but if I found that some did not teach what is sound (like those that follow the Children of God), I warned the local believers. I told them that if they continued in it, they would lose their souls and deceive others.

I knew of a man who, after having been with me for twenty-six years, became a Jehovah's Witness. He received three years' imprisonment. I was compelled to write to all the churches, telling them not to have any fellowship with him. So he was cut off and all alone. He fasted and prayed that Brother Prem might understand that Jehovah is God and Creator. But when I tried to meet him, he would not meet with me and he moved to Pocra.

As I have said, because Pocra is a tourist center, I am losing more people there. Many are deceived by the so-called

tourists who are really missionaries. They are sent by foreign missions who are anxious to have a work in Nepal. I
have no hard feelings against any man; but still, that is the
way they do their work.

Just before my second imprisonment, one of my
brothers from the church tried to form a group with an
American man. This American met with us all the time.
He worked for three years in Nepal through the American
Embassy as an agricultural specialist. He came regularly
to our worship services in Katmandu with his wife and
children.

Just before this family left Nepal at the end of his con-
tract, he brought a man from India who was a Church of
Christ missionary. The missionary, along with the other
brother, questioned me about when a man is actually
saved. I replied that a man is saved when he accepts Jesus
Christ as his Savior. We talked back and forth for about
five or six hours, quoting verses from the Bible to support
our opposing positions. There was no settlement of the
issue. Finally, I suggested that we stop the discussion and
each should keep his own faith on the matter. Neither one
of us was able to convince the other, and I did not want to
argue about it. So we went our separate ways.

This brother (the agricultural specialist) brought three
other brothers to talk to me again. They were elders from
his church in Denver, Colorado. They tried to convert me

to their beliefs, the doctrines of the Church of Christ. I told them what I believed. They told me their beliefs. Still there was no agreement, and finally they left.

8

Loss of Property in Katmandu from Betrayal

During my first imprisonment, a prisoner called Basu became a Christian. He was a political prisoner. After his release, he worked for the Lord and translated the whole Gospel of John. He did good work. I relied on him and trusted him with whatever finances I had so that he could give it to other brothers who needed support in the Lord's work. He knew all the leading brothers.

When the head of his political party was released and went to India, brother Basu also left for India to join his party. He continued the political work there for three years, but he kept the faith. Later on, when the head of the political party returned to Nepal, Basu also returned. He was put in prison along with many others. He was imprisoned for another three years.

When I was released from my first imprisonment, my school in Katmandu was closed by the government, because many were becoming Christians there. Brother Basu told me that the government could take the school building and all that I had because it was in my name, so he suggested that I turn the land and the building over to his wife's name and when needed, the property would be transferred back to me. This would save it from the hands of the government.

In our country, if the church bought some land and built a school building, the property was not in the church's name but in an individual's name. The school and the property in Katmandu were in my name. I took Brother Basu's advice and transferred it to his wife's name.

I trusted Basu because I had known him for a long time. While he was in prison with me and was converted, his wife was kicked out of their home along with their little child. I sent them to live in my home with my wife. After my release from prison, Basu and his wife ended up living with my wife and me for more than eighteen years. We ate together and lived together and I loved him deeply. He and his wife did good work. They helped me with administrative work for the school and with the farm work.

You can understand my distress when, about five months ago, my beloved brother Basu sold the building. This is a large three-story building that was used as the Bible school and a place for Christians to stay. Many Christians lived together in that building. Basu and his wife have subsequently renounced their Christian faith.

He renewed his Hindu vows and is worshipping in the Hindu temple. Even their children (two daughters and a son), who grew up with me and whom I love as much as my own children, have followed their parents and returned to the Hindu faith.

Not only that, Basu has also given the names of all the Christian leaders to the government and reported the way I am working with churches and how I am helping them with money. That is why the government has learned perfectly, now, that I am the man who is responsible behind all Christian work. As a result, the government has arrested many and is now searching for me. I hid for three months, and then I came over to Canada to speak in the churches, as this trip had been scheduled for a long time.

Yes, Basu did much harm to the church. Like the Apostle Paul, I have to say that not only has this brother betrayed the faith, but he has done me a great deal of harm. However, I cannot judge him or do anything against him but pray. Basu has been disfellowshipped from the churches because he is not a Christian anymore and lives in his own way as a Hindu.

Actually, the loss of the building and the property was entirely my fault. Many of the brothers who were elders told me all the time that they did not trust Basu because he was a political man and his background was in politics. Maybe they saw something in him that I did not. When they told me about him, I did not take it seriously. Now I know it was my fault for trusting this brother so much.

This whole matter has been very painful to me. If Basu had just sold the building and had not betrayed the Christians, it would not have been so bad; but now because of him, many brothers and sisters have been put in prison. In many areas, the places where Christians met to worship were compelled to be shut down. Now, two or three Christian families worship together in one home and two or three in another home, and they change the location daily. The Christians who meet in homes might be next door to Hindu and Buddhist homes, so they sing quietly.

Many Christians are now in hiding, and they have difficulty living in the forests because there is not much food. This has brought much pain to my heart, but I find one consolation. Although the government has put so much pressure on the church, still she is growing. Where fifty, sixty or a hundred people would meet to worship in one place, now they are meeting in twenty different places. The people continue bringing their sick to places where Christians meet. As God heals the sick, the church continues to grow.

Gene Edwards: It has been the most interesting thing, hearing Prem tell of all the suffering he has known at the hands of the government and the blessings God has worked, but the Cross in Prem's life goes on. You do not ever earn freedom from the Cross. In fact, it seems that sometimes it just becomes more and more intense. If anyone had the right to live well or die well for what he gave for the Lord, it would be John the Baptist; and if any brother would be excused from any more agony of the soul, surely Brother Prem would graduate now... if we could graduate.

Although I have gone through much persecution from the government and also some from the religious organizations, yet the most painful experience of all was the betrayal of Basu. Basu became a part of me, sharing my own thinking and my teaching in the church. He was a member of the church, so what he did to me was much more painful than what any outsiders could do. Those from organized denominations have their own way of thinking and will do things against my work because they do not see the truth. That does not hurt me as much as one of my very own brothers and my convert.

Prem's Comments on Persecution of the Church

In spite of the suffering and the persecution from without and within, the church is growing. I have taught the other brothers not to be discouraged, because whatever persecution we go through is for the furtherance of the gospel. We can surely give thanks to God for that.

Many people tell me, "Brother Prem, we will pray for the government to change the law of your country." I have asked them not to pray in that way. If the law changes, everyone will be free to go to Nepal as missionaries. Then there will be many denominations in Nepal, as there are in the West. The church in Nepal would become a weak church. I read about the time in Rome when Constantine ordered all his subjects to become Christians and they did, but from that moment on, the church became weak. If the law changes in Nepal, our church will also become weak, and that is not good. It is good that persecution remains and the Christians are good Christians. Suffering is good for them and will make them strong. Instead of changing the law of the country, it is better to change hearts to be willing to suffer and see the church increase. The church will be strong and will be prepared for heaven.

Gene Edwards: When the world persecutes you, the church can have a certain rejoicing. It is the most obvious confrontation from the enemy. When the religious system persecutes you, you will feel it much more deeply. Especially will those in leadership feel it. God's people may not particularly feel that. The only way they will feel that pain is when the leaders feed it to them. A worker must never do that. If you do, you are not worthy to be a worker, because what you are doing is feeding hate to your people. This is a very powerful tool and does marvelous, wonderful things, but none of them are godly. None of them are in Christ Jesus. It has been my observation for about forty years now (especially the brothers I know outside the organized church) that when they are persecuted, they sink. If it is not immorality, it is money by which these men get eliminated early on. But there are the men who go on with the Lord and shepherd God's people, taking what the world and the Christian community have to throw at them. Most of those who have either been destroyed or embittered have ended up that way because it has come from pain inflicted within the fellowship! That gets closer to the heart. There are very few things that cause so much pain as Christians within the fellowship betraying you. But do not return evil for evil. It just does not matter what the issue is. It can be immorality, false doctrine, lies or twisted truth. It does not matter what it is. Do not inflict pain on another child of God. Remember, we are one body. If you hurt a brother, it is as if you take a dagger and throw it into his heart. I would not be wise to take a knife in my right hand and stab my left arm.

But that is not the issue either. You are taking a dagger in your right hand and you are stabbing your Savior and your Lord. It is not just one body, it is His body. If there is anything that should be sacred among us, it is loving one another. If you simply cannot love, try to find some way to remove yourself from the situation, but do not do hurtful things in bitterness. Expect such things to happen. As much as we will implore you to never do it, for sure, somebody is going to do it, probably to you. Just make sure it is not you who does it.

9

Prem Speaks to Christian Workers in the West

Prem Pradhan's Trip to America

About six months after my release from my third imprisonment, I came to America and visited churches.

I shared with the churches something of my experiences in the prison and what God is doing in my country. I especially tried to tell the Christians in the United States what they needed to hear. I told them the things on my heart concerning the church. I also told them that the truth was, the Christians were only serving their organizations, not Jesus. I did not find many people actually working for the Lord, winning souls and establishing churches. The Christians here were satisfied with whatever organization or denomination to which they belonged. Some did not even know if they were Christians, but they were in the church.

Wherever I went to visit churches, I tried to tell them that they needed the Savior to save their souls and that when they became Christians, God had a purpose for their lives. He wanted them to win others and to establish churches and God's kingdom on this earth.

Also, I would try to raise the level of people's faith among the different kinds of churches where I spoke. I would tell them that if they are one body, then they must work as one. But if they said they were one body and yet did not love one another, then there was no proof in what they said. If they did not do the things God told them to do and were simply satisfied that their souls were saved (some of them were saved), then they missed out on the purpose for why God saved them.

I shared these things with the churches where I traveled in Canada. I tried to help the people understand the Body of Christ: why Jesus died and through His blood made one body. I taught this so that people who came into this knowledge might live according to the way God has shown in the Bible.

Gene Edwards: There was a time, when the gospel was planted in Ireland, and then later the church became so corrupt that evangelical Christians moved to an island called lona and they preached the gospel for several hundred years. They not only traveled to where the gospel had never been preached, but they even traveled all the way from Scotland to Rome to re-preach the gospel to a people who had forgotten what it was. That was back in 500 AD. Here is a brother coming to us from Nepal with something as simple as salvation and the church, because he feels this is what this country needs. I think that is rather remarkable.

Regarding Healing

In the West, the men who pray for the sick advertise and get a lot of publicity. God is not honored as the one who alone should receive all honor. Also, here in America, people follow men, and so they quench the Spirit. God is not allowed to work.

Every Christian is a member of the body, and God works through the body. A local body of Christians might be just ten or fifteen people, but if they have faith to pray and ask God to do something for the sick, he will do it, even in your country.

In Philadelphia, I stayed with a brother who lived near a Baptist church and seminary. The church had a meeting one Saturday in the basement of their building, and one of the six pastors of that Baptist church invited me to speak. A lady who heard me speak came after the meeting and asked me to pray for her arm that had been paralyzed.

I prayed, and God healed her. She rejoiced and went home. Her husband was a member of the faculty of the Baptist Bible Seminary. That Sunday they faced much trouble because of the lady's healing. The pastors held a meeting to ask me how I healed that lady. I told them that I did not heal, but Jesus did; I had simply prayed. They criticized me and said that it was not in their theology. I replied that I did not know any theology, but I knew Jesus. I left that place.

The pastor who had invited me was discharged and came to see me. I encouraged him and told him that if he opened his home, I would spend fifteen days with him. Every day we had meetings in his home. Very few came, for many were afraid to come. We preached and prayed, and God helped us. Slowly the group grew larger and they rented a place to meet and start a church. The church grew and did well, because they followed in the New Testament pattern and believed in God always.

Another brother, who lived in Indiana, was almost blind. He came to a meeting where I spoke in Chicago, Illinois and I prayed for his eyes. He was completely healed. He worked in the Bell Telephone Company for twenty years and has now retired.

A woman in Philadelphia was healed of breast cancer. When her doctor learned that his patient was healed, he came to see me in Chicago. He was not a Christian, but he asked me to pray for his son who had incurred some brain damage in a snowball fight with friends. His son was out of school, for he could do nothing. I drove with this doctor all the way back to his home at night. When we arrived, his son was asleep. I prayed for him and went back that same night because I had a meeting scheduled elsewhere. Later, when I had a meeting in San Francisco, that same doctor came to see me. He told me that his son was healed and that he had become a Christian. God is doing things like that all the time.

Here in America, people do not have faith to believe God can heal. They rely too much on what they see and feel. When people find that the pain is still there, they conclude that they are not healed. Man goes more by feeling than by believing.

I will give you a personal example. Back in Nepal, it is not uncommon to see lizards on our ceilings. One day, while my wife was looking after the children, she fell asleep. When she opened her eyes, one of the lizards fell into her eye and caused it to burn with pain. I was sleeping in the barn outside the house, and I came in to wash her eye. It continued to burn with pain after that. I prayed for her and she fell asleep. In the morning the eye was all swollen and white. I took her to the hospital that was 150 miles away. The doctor gave her some medicine to try and treat it. We stayed in that hospital for seven days. When my wife's eye showed no sign of improvement, the doctor advised us to go for further treatment in a big hospital that treated eyes. That was in the capital city of Katmandu. We went and after another fifteen days of treatment and further medication, she was cured of all the swelling and pain; however, a black spot remained, and she could not see anything out of that eye. The doctor recommended an eye graft. He gave us a letter to take to the hospital in Lucknow, India.

I sent my wife to India with other brothers and sisters. She went through a series of eye examinations and was told to wait, because there were no eyes available for grafting. The doctor said that even if my wife's eye was grafted, there was no guarantee that it would work, because it might be rejected. When she returned home within four days, I found that her eye was still in the same condition. Nothing had changed. I asked her why she came back. She told me that the doctor had sent her back and had asked me to pray for her. I told my wife that I had prayed for her already. She said that nothing had changed. So I said that I would pray for her again.

I prayed again and again. I asked my wife if she could see little things, like the many colors on the carpet. I told her that she must first give thanks as I prayed God would heal her. She looked at the carpet and said that she could not see . . . but she had not given thanks. Then she went outside the house and looked at the bright noonday sun.

She came back and told me that she could barely see the light. I told her she must give thanks that she could see light.

My wife gave thanks for seeing a little light of the sun. I too gave thanks continually. After several days she woke up one morning and could see the colors of the carpet, blue and yellow and so on. I told my wife that now she must give thanks that God had healed her, and I told her that she would surely be all right if she just believed. Within four days the black spot in her eye was completely gone and she was healed.

I sent my wife back to the doctor in Katmandu who had all the medical records. He examined her and could not understand how her eye was healed, because no grafting had been done. My wife explained how the doctor in India had sent her home to ask me to pray for her. The doctor was greatly surprised to find out that my wife was healed by prayer alone, no medication or treatment. He tested her eyes and found that the one which had been bad was completely well, and the other eye that was good needed glasses.

You see, now, that we must not rely on our feelings alone. If we believe that Jesus is the same yesterday, today, and forever, he can do the same work today as ever before. Our only work is that we must believe. That is the difference between people here in the West and the believers in

126

Nepal. The sick in Nepal go to their Hindu and Buddhist gods in temples to seek help and relief from their illnesses. In a way, that is one reason why they have faith when they become Christians. Here in the West, people put too much faith in doctors.

The Danger of Honoring Man Rather Than God in Miracles of Healing

Whether doctors or healers bring about healing, we must not get mixed up with attributing more honor to the instrument which God uses to bring healing than we do to God Himself. All the glory must be given to God. It is very difficult for people not to be puffed up when God uses them. They start thinking about their gift and the fact that they can heal, instead of honoring God.

You must always remember that I cannot heal anyone. Only Jesus Himself can heal.

If we should feel even once that we can do anything, that means we will lose. God is not going to allow us to be used if we do that.

People have suggested that I should take a cassette player with taped messages of the gospel to share with the people. That would not work because it could not heal anyone. What we have said we must do, or people will not receive the message. If I preach that Jesus Christ is alive and that He is the same yesterday, today and forever and He can heal people now, then when I am asked to pray for the sick, I can do so. And Jesus does heal. That is a much better way to work than to carry a cassette player with taped messages.

In this country, I know good brothers who are prominent in the Christian ministry and have invited me to speak in their meetings. Nevertheless, I was grieved when I saw a pamphlet that advertised a special healing meeting. It was an invitation to come to a breakfast meeting at $100 a ticket. I made a protest to the brother who was to minister at that meeting. I told him that I could no longer speak in his meetings, because only rich people could be healed. What about the poor?

I am sorry to say this about a good brother who is a Christian. The devil is very cunning. He tries to destroy those who are used by the Lord by causing them to have pride in their hearts. That is why I do not like to talk much about healing in public meetings. I want to inspire people to have faith, so I do share with them the testimonies of healing. Otherwise, I do not like to talk about it. All I say is that God heals, but I do not give details.

Regarding Leadership and Authority

Within the church, no one has ever questioned my authority. So far, no one has said that they can do a better job than I do and that they want to be in charge. It has not happened yet, but someday it will happen after I die.

In America, there is already an existing problem with leadership because of the culture and the divisions. Very few people here truly understand that the body is one and that Christ is the head. He controls the leader and everyone of His members. Most of the people have this knowledge in their head, but they do not apply it to practical things. If we practice what the Bible teaches, then every man will surely respect his own brother who is leading the work, because the Word of God tells us to hold in honor and respect those who teach the brethren.

Brother Bakht Singh has never had the problem of his authority's being challenged in India because he established the church there. He is the church's apostle or prophet. In Nepal the Lord led me and helped me to establish the church. There was no one before me. I was Nepal's first native worker. That is why churches there have a different stand regarding me. But in other countries, things are not that way.

I want to say that in America it is possible to have a work like the work I had in Nepal. There is no difference, because we have the same God and the same Spirit who works through us. Here, when you convert people, you have to train them to follow you. If they learn from the beginning what the New Testament pattern is, they will not stray away to some other practice.

There are so many difficulties in America because every man wants to be the leader, but he does not wish to pay the price of suffering. If someone is a real worker, he will face suffering, even here in America. Scripture tells us that anyone who lives a godly life will suffer persecution. Elsewhere it is written that it has been given unto us on behalf of Christ not only to believe on Him but also to suffer for His sake.

A few days ago I met a young man from a Jewish family who became a Christian. His whole family stood against him. The pastor of the church where I was speaking asked me after the meeting if I would encourage him. I talked to this young man and prayed with him. He told me how even his own wife was no longer willing to stay with him. So that kind of suffering is not peculiar to Nepal alone; it is over here, too.

Possible Problems of the Work in Nepal after Prem's Death

I have been in the work of establishing churches for over 35 years, so the foundation has been well laid. I do not fear that it will collapse after my death. It will go on. There might be another man to take the place of Brother

Bakht Singh after his death; and for myself, I will prepare a man before that time comes.

It will be good for me to give up the work when I hand it over to another man. I could be watching the work from outside while giving it spiritual leadership. If I participated with him and I said one word and perhaps everybody who heard it followed me, it would create disunity. So, it is necessary to stay outside of the work but to watch over it and to help the church by preparing someone else. If the man who was being prepared is doing a good work, then he would not need any input from me. If not, then I can step in to correct him though it might be a very difficult thing to do.

Denominations were started because when the leader died, everything went in the wrong direction. My only hope is that the church in Nepal will not become a denomination. There might be those who would come and take some of our brothers to establish a denomination. The religious groups have a lot of money, and a good brother can be turned back from the pattern of work which was started. After my death, some may go and start a denomination, but I am not responsible for that.

A man called J.U. told me that I would not be able to keep all the people with me all the time because he had money. I told him that it might be true, but what profit would there be in splitting the church? He said that even if

I identified believers as "only Christians" in Nepal, that too would be a denomination of Only Christians. Everywhere believers would be known by that term. Also if I went to other countries and taught them the same thing, then I might start a movement called Only Christians. And if other brothers from my group in Nepal started churches like I did in different areas and called them "only Christians," then everywhere, churches that were started would be called, Only Christians.

I did not agree with what this brother said. I told him that I did not agree with denominations and that my work would never become a denomination. He insisted that it would be. I do not think it needs to be that way at all.

We are responsible for our lifetime on this earth. We are responsible to be faithful to God and not to have a denomination while we live on this earth. After our death, we are no longer responsible. What will happen to the work after I am gone, I do not know. Jesus paid the price of his own blood, and He established His own church. It is His church.

After me, I believe that the Lord has to raise up a man to continue my work. The people may have some problems for a little while, but they will surely understand that we, as workers, leave behind a principle after death. We leave a clear-cut vision to the people that will not die. I may die, but the things that are put into the hearts of men will not die. Surely God will raise up someone with the same vision in his heart that is also in mine.

If there has to be a denomination, it must first be written in the Bible. Everything is written by the Spirit of God, and whatever I need to know, I find it written in God's Word. When it is not written there, then I cannot agree, and we will never ever need to have a denomination. If there is a denomination, then it is made by man and not God. Paul said to the Corinthians, some of you are saying: I am of Paul, I am of Apollos, I am of Peter. We are just workers. Some sow seed and others water it, but it is God who gives the growth. So we are one. We do not say: this is Paul's denomination and this is Peter's or Apollos' denomination. There is nothing in the Word that says we must have a denomination.

I pray that God will keep at least one country in truth, one nation on earth that has no organized church

A Major Crisis in Prem's Life Is Resolved

If I am sent to prison again, the government cannot confiscate my property. The only crime that could cause me to lose everything would be that I went against the king. I have not baptized anyone for the last ten years, because the elders would not allow me to do so. They do not want to see me in prison again.

The only way the Nepalese government could place charges against me would be through my preaching of the gospel. That would be hard to prove unless one of the Christians witnessed that I talked to people and reported that to the authorities.

Last night I was in my room reading the Bible (the book of Numbers) where Moses was taking the Israelites to find water. The Lord told Moses to take the rod in his hand, gather all the people together, and speak to the rock to bring forth water. All the time that Moses was caring for the people, they were murmuring and rebelling against him. Caring for the people and their burdens was too much for him, and he became weary. Moses gathered the people together as God commanded, but instead of speaking to the rock to bring forth water, he struck it twice with the rod.

Moses' heart was always so burdened for the people. Many times God wanted to kill all the Israelites and build a nation out of Moses, but he pleaded for the people and God heard his prayer. But now he was angry with the people because of their rebellion. Moses was a man, and he struck the rock. Although water came out of the rock when Moses struck it, he did not do what was right.

I started thinking of my own situation: I lead the people, they have no one. I do all my best to help them, pray for them and lead them. Something suddenly came to my mind about the thing that was done after the building in Katmandu was taken away from me. It was my mistake to entrust this house in the name of the brother who sold it. I held on to this house for four months after it was sold and did not allow the new owner to move in. Last night,.I felt in my heart that the man who bought the house did nothing wrong. He bought it legally. I had told the students in the Bible school not to leave the house, and they obeyed me. Whenever the new owners would come to ask the students to leave the house, they remained because I had told them to do so. I should have given it up when it was sold. Will God punish me as he punished Moses?

I prayed about it and God showed me to give the house back to the man who bought it. It was a difficult thing, and my flesh wanted to hold onto it. The ground floor was rented for $300 a month, and that helped to support my brothers in the work. The second floor was kept for the students who went to college, and they stayed there and had their Bible studies there. The third floor was where I had the Bible classes, and it had a kitchen in it. So the house was used for a lot of things.

Also, my mind was on the loan given by Christian Aid for the work in Nepal, as well as the loans in my own country for the work on the farm. With all the loans owed already and the pressure of trying to get the house back, it made it all too much for me. I felt moved to put all these things into the hands of the Lord, and I spent most of the night in prayer.

I realized that it was not good for me to hold on to that building. As a Christian, it was wrong on my part to give trouble to this businessman who bought the building for use as offices. So I decided to give the building to him.

A great peace came over me, confirming what was in my own heart. I may lose the house, but by making this decision I have peace in my heart, and much of the burden is gone from me.

I have decided that I need to return to Nepal to take care of the things that are in that house and to vacate it. The brothers in Nepal have asked me not to enter Nepal. They will report to me the things that happen there. However, I feel I need to return to Katmandu to take care of the matters relating to the house. Then, if necessary, I will go into hiding. If not, I can visit the churches and the many Christians that are in police custody or in prison. I could send them food and other things through other men, but if I see them and visit them in person, they receive much joy and encouragement.

Publisher's Note: Prem went back to Nepal in 1990, and did not sue for regaining ownership of the house. He found that foreign missionaries had taken over his work in total. He started over from scratch and continued the work of planting indigenous Nepali churches until his death in 1998. A ruptured aorta caused his death while he was in the Himalayan Mountains planting churches where western men had never traveled.

A Final Word
by Gene Edwards:

The quality of Prem's life, his suffering which came about because of the high quality of the churches he planted, is unmatched and unprecedented in church history. As a church planter he was peerless. The courage he exhibited in planting those churches is without parallel. It is reserved to this man to have set a standard to which Christian workers must repair.

Finally, the persecution at the hands of modern missionaries is living proof that the institutional church is as ruthless, as dangerous, as unprincipled today as it was in the dark ages. Let it be known that the beautiful facade of today's church, when even slightly threatened, is as vicious, cruel, and dishonest as it has always been. Prem's response to that fact was courage in the face of cowardice, truth in the face of lies, and power in the face of tradition. His life also teaches us the same lesson we find in the lives of such men throughout the ages, and that is that they face constant betrayal from within.

We may never see the likes of this man again, but let Christian workers measure their lives by his devotion. He was a church planter extraordinaire, without equal. He has given us the definition of what a church planter is and what is to be expected of those who would dare serve the Lord, utterly outside the traditional Christianity.

Prem Pradhan

Maya, Prem's wife

SEEDSOWERS
800-228-2665   (fax) 866-252-5504
www.seedsowers.com

REVOLUTIONARY BOOKS ON CHURCH LIFE

Beyond Radical *(Edwards)* 8.95
How to Meet In Homes *(Edwards)* 10.95
The Christian Woman...Set Free*(Edwards)* 12.95
When the Church Was Led Only by Laymen *(Edwards)* 5.00
Revolution, The Story of the Early Church *(Edwards)* 12.95
The Silas Diary *(Edwards)* 10.95
The Titus Diary *(Edwards)* 10.95
The Timothy Diary *(Edwards)* 10.95
The Priscilla Diary *(Edwards)* 10.95
The Gaius Diary *(Edwards)* 10.95
Overlooked Christianity *(Edwards)* 10.95
Paul's Way or the Seminary's Way *(Edwards)* 12.95
The Shocking Story of the History of Bible Study *(Edwards)* .... coming soon
Why You Should Consider Leaving the Pastorate *(Edwards)* 5.00
The Organic Church vs. The New Testament Church *(Edwards)* 7.50
Problems and Solutions in a House Church *(Edwards)* 7.50
How to Start a House Church From Scratch *(Edwards)* 5.00
Why So Many House Churches Fail and What to Do About It *(Edwards)* 5.00

AN INTRODUCTION TO THE DEEPER CHRISTIAN LIFE

Living by the Highest Life *(Edwards)* 10.95
The Secret to the Christian Life *(Edwards)* 10.95
The Inward Journey *(Edwards)* 12.95

CLASSICS ON THE DEEPER CHRISTIAN LIFE

Experiencing the Depths of Jesus Christ *(Guyon)* 9.95
Practicing His Presence *(Lawrence/Laubach)* 9.95
The Spiritual Guide *(Molinos)* 9.95
Union With God *(Guyon)* 9.95
The Seeking Heart *(Fenelon)* 10.95
Intimacy with Christ *(Guyon)* 10.95
Spiritual Torrents *(Guyon)* 10.95
The Ultimate Intention *(Fromke)* 10.00
One Hundred Days in the Secret Place *(Edwards)* 13.99

IN A CLASS BY ITSELF

The Divine Romance *(Edwards)* 12.99

NEW TESTAMENT

The Story of My Life as Told by Jesus Christ *(Four gospels blended)* 14.95
The Day I was Crucified as Told by Jesus the Christ 14.99
Acts in First Person *(Book of Acts)* 9.95

COMMENTARIES BY JEANNE GUYON

Genesis Commentary 10.95
Exodus Commentary 10.95
Leviticus - Numbers - Deuteronomy Commentaries 12.95
Judges Commentary 7.95
Job Commentary 10.95
Song of Songs *(Song of Solomon Commentary)* 9.95

(2008 prices...subject to change later)

COMMENTARIES BY JEANNE GUYON CONTINUED

Jeremiah Commentary 7.95
James - I John - Revelation Commentaries 12.95

THE CHRONICLES OF HEAVEN (Edwards)

Christ Before Creation 8.99
The Beginning 8.99
The Escape 8.99
The Birth 8.99
The Triumph 8.99
The Return 8.99

THE COLLECTED WORKS OF T. AUSTIN-SPARKS

The Centrality of Jesus Christ 19.95
The House of God 29.95
Ministry 29.95
Service 19.95
Spiritual Foundations 29.95
The Things of the Spirit 10.95
Prayer 14.95
The On-High Calling 10.95
Rivers of Living Water 8.95
The Power of His Resurrection 8.95

COMFORT AND HEALING

A Tale of Three Kings (Edwards) 8.99
The Prisoner in the Third Cell (Edwards) 9.99
Letters to a Devastated Christian (Edwards) 8.95
Exquisite Agony (Edwards) 9.95
Dear Lillian (Edwards) paperback 5.95
Dear Lillian (Edwards) hardcover 9.99

OTHER BOOKS ON CHURCH LIFE

Climb the Highest Mountain (Edwards) 12.95
The Torch of the Testimony (Kennedy) 14.95
The Passing of the Torch (Chen) 9.95
Going to Church in the First Century (Banks) 6.95
When the Church was Young (Loosley) 8.95
Church Unity (Litzman,Nee,Edwards) 10.95
Let's Return to Christian Unity (Kurosaki) 10.95

CHRISTIAN LIVING

The Christian Woman . . . Set Free (Edwards) 12.95
Your Lord Is a Blue Collar Worker (Edwards) 7.95
The Autobiography of Jeanne Guyon 19.95
Final Steps in Christian Maturity (Guyon) 12.95
Turkeys and Eagles (Lord) 9.95
The Life of Jeanne Guyon (T.C. Upham) 17.95
Abridged Edition of Guyon's Autobiography (Johnson) 10.95
All and Only (Kilpatrick) 8.95
Adoration (Kilpatrick) 9.95
Bone of His Bone (Huegel) modernized 9.95
You Can Witness with Confidence (Rinker) 10.95